THE LOLLARDS OF THE
CHILTERN HILLS

AMS PRESS
NEW YORK

THE LOLLARDS OF THE CHILTERN HILLS

Glimpses of English Dissent in the Middle Ages

By

W. H. SUMMERS

Author of "Our Lollard Ancestors," "Memories of Jordans
and the Chalfonts," &c.

LONDON

FRANCIS GRIFFITHS

34 Maiden Lane, Strand, W.C.

1906

Library of Congress Cataloging in Publication Data

Summers, William Henry.
The Lollards of the Chiltern Hills.

Reprint of the 1906 ed. published by F. Griffiths,
London.
1. Lollards. 2. England—Church history—Medieval
period, 1066-1485. I. Title.
BX4901.S85 1980   274.25   80-12770
ISBN 0-404-16245-2

MANUFACTURED
IN THE UNITED STATES OF AMERICA

CONTENTS

———

PREFACE

In the following pages, an attempt has been made to illustrate from the records of a single county the course of a religious movement the influence of which upon the story of the English people has been much more deep and far-reaching than is usually supposed.

The writer was first led to take up the subject by the interest he felt in listening to curious local traditions of the Lollard times, still extant in the old abodes of the " Known Men " in Buckinghamshire, while he was for several years a resident in the district. In the year 1888, a series of articles from his pen, upon the " Lollards of Bucks," appeared in a local paper, the *South Bucks Free Press*. But he was then under the great disadvantage of being dependent for nearly all his facts upon the statements of that much discredited writer, John Foxe, and was not aware to what a remarkable extent Foxe's statements, with regard to Buckinghamshire at any rate, are confirmed and illustrated by independent authorities.

A very large number of writers have been consulted in the preparation of the work; and in most cases the names of these are given. But as the work is intended for popular use, extracts from the Latin are given in an English translation, and old English is modernised where it is likely to present a difficulty. The references to books and documents, however, will enable those who wish to do so to consult the original text for themselves.

Some of the matter contained in the earlier chapters may at first sight seem somewhat irrelevant, as relating to North Bucks, where Lollardy never appears to have gained a footing; but it will be found that these passages often refer to institutions and localities to which allusion is made in the later chapters.

In conclusion, the writer desires to express his obligation to a number of gentlemen who have assisted him with valuable information and suggestions. Among these he may mention Mr. C. Guthrie, K.C., Procurator of the United Free Church of Scotland; the late Rev. P. W. Phipps, M.A., rector of Chalfont St. Giles; Mr. J. Cheese, of Amersham; and especially Dr. F. J. Furnivall, who has allowed him to make use of some "confessions of heresy," copied for the use of the Early English Text Society, though unfortunately not yet published in a complete form, owing to the scanty support accorded by the public to that excellent organisation.

The Lollards of the Chiltern Hills

CHAPTER I

SAINTLY LEGENDS

" Now it is no small praise to Buckinghamshire, that being one of the lesser counties of England, it had more martyrs and confessors in it before the time of Luther than all the kingdom besides."

So says Thomas Fuller (*Church History*, book v., chap. i.) ; and though his statement is perhaps not literally correct, it may fitly serve to introduce the story of the Buckinghamshire Lollards. Before entering on that story, however, it may be well to sketch the earlier conditions of religious life among which they arose.

Scarcely any traditions survive of the introduction of the faith of Christ into this part of England. Some have seen a memorial of Saxon, if not of Celtic, piety, in the crosses cut out in the turf of the Chiltern Hills at Whiteleaf and Bledlow, above the ancient British road of the Icknield Way. But these are probably of far later origin; though the Puritan dislike to the sign of the cross makes it difficult to accept the suggestion of the late Mr. E. J. Payne that the Whiteleaf Cross was a landmark cut out by the Parliamentary soldiers.

The Rev. T. Williams, in an interesting article in the *Records of Buckinghamshire* for 1896, considers it likely that the earliest apostle of the county in Saxon days was Birinus, the founder of the see of Dorchester (Oxon), whose name survives in Berin's Hill, near Ipsden, five or six miles from the county boundary, where he is said to have had a cell, and perhaps in Bicester (Buringceastre). He died, says the legend, from the bite of an adder on the Chiltern Hills, upon December 3rd, 650. (Adders did not hybernate in those days, it would seem!)

The Chiltern country, then and for centuries after, was a vast forest of beeches and other trees, the haunt of the wolf, the boar, and the wild ox, and of robbers and outlaws yet more dreaded. The credit of making the forest passable for wayfarers is given to Leofstan, Abbot of St. Albans, in the days of Edward the Confessor. He opened up roads, and appointed men-at-arms to patrol the forest. It was the need of guarding this wild region that gave rise to the well-known office of "steward of the Chiltern Hundreds." But the wild and beautiful scenery which characterises South Bucks fostered good as well as evil elements of character. Alike in the days of the Lollards, in

the Reformation period, and in the days of the
Civil War, the men of the Chiltern Hundreds,
John Hampden's country, were foremost in the
struggle against civil and ecclesiastical despotism,
while those of the flatter district to the north
of the hills were, as a rule, more disposed to
yield to constituted authority.

When Birinus landed in 634, only fifty-four
years had elapsed since the Saxons took
Aylesbury. But it is quite uncertain whether
any relics of British Christianity remained, and
certainly heathenism was fully established in the
district. Mr. Payne, in an article in Gibbs'
Buckinghamshire Miscellany, thinks that Woden
was worshipped at Waddesdon, Thor at Turville,
Hilda at Hillesden, and Ægil, the sun-god, at
Aylesbury. Mr. Williams, however, derives the
name of the county town from the British *Eglwys*,
a church, and thinks that one already stood there.
Soon, at any rate, the county was so far Chris-
tianised as to have saints of its own. Prominent
among these was that marvellous infant St.
Rumbold or Romwald, a grandchild of Penda of
Mercia, born at King's Sutton in Northamptonshire, but buried at Buckingham. The legend,
quaintly and contemptuously told by Fuller in
his *Worthies of England*, narrates how he cried
three times, "I am a Christian," as soon as he
was born; how he asked to be baptized, choosing
his name and god-parents; how he pointed out
a hollow stone to be used as the font, which none
but his godfathers were able to lift; how he

spent three days in pious discourse, and then died, having ordered that his body should remain at Sutton one year, at Brackley two years, and at Buckingham ever after. The fame of the child-saint spread far and wide, and in the Middle Ages his shrine in Buckingham parish church was the resort of numerous pilgrims, for whose accommodation a large hostelry known as "Pilgrim's Inn," which was standing at the close of the eighteenth century, was erected. The town had a "St. Rumbold's Street," and a "Guild of St. Rumbold," incorporated by Henry VI.; and also several holy wells, the supposed efficacy of which in healing the blind and the lame was ascribed to the merits of the saint. There were also "Wells of St. Rumbold" at King's Sutton and Brackley, and a famous image of him at Bexley in Kent. This last, like the Holy Grail that Sir Lancelot might not see, was a test of chastity, for none but the pure in heart and life could lift it. The fact was, it is said, that it was fastened by a peg behind, which was only removed for those who had been liberal enough in their offerings.

Aylesbury, as well as Buckingham, had its saints in Saxon times. Eadburg and Eaditha, the daughters of Frithwald, a Mercian under-king, are said to have received Aylesbury as a gift from their father, and to have taken the veil in a convent there. St. Eadburg died at Aylesbury, but her body was afterwards removed to Edburton in Suffolk, where miracles were said to have been wrought at her tomb. The story of St. Osyth or Sithe, sister or niece of Eadburg and Eaditha, comes before us in a most shadowy form. She is said to have been born at Quarrendon, at a period variously stated; to have been educated at Ellesborough; to have been compelled by her father to marry Sigebert, King of East Anglia; to have taken the veil, and founded St. Osyth's monastery, near Colchester, where she remained as abbess for many years; and to have been beheaded by Danish pirates. The corpse of the virgin martyr was brought to Aylesbury, remained there and worked miracles for forty-six years, and was then taken back to St. Osyth's Abbey, the fear of Danish incursions having ceased for a time. At Bierton, close to Aylesbury, was a well of St. Osyth, now known as " Up Town Well."

The old chronicler Roger of Wendover tells of a St. Ulfric or Wulfric, who lived at Aylesbury (unless Aylesbeere in Devonshire is really meant), under Henry I., but was of Saxon blood. From being a worldly priest, fond of his hawks and hounds, he became a rigorous ascetic, clad in a single hair-cloth garment or iron cuirass, eating no flesh, and speaking to no one save through a grated window. We are told that by his sanctity and prayers he even rescued an unhappy north-countryman, who had sold his soul to the enemy of mankind !

Another Saxon saint who became the object of special reverence in Buckinghamshire was Wulstan, Bishop of Worcester, who, in consideration of his fidelity to William the Conqueror, was allowed to retain his diocese after the other Saxon bishops had been deprived, and was reverenced throughout the country as a living link with the days of Edward the Confessor. In 1076, however, he was cited before a great council at Westminster, as " insufficient for his place for want of learning." On his way, he passed through High Wycombe. The house in which he lodged being in an insecure condition, an alarm was raised that it was giving way, and his servants rushed forth in terror. Wulstan, however, remained to the last, and quietly left the house just before it fell. An exhibition of self-control like this seemed nothing short of miraculous to that superstitious age, but it was fully in keeping with his conduct before the council. He was declared incapable of exercising his functions, and was summoned by William to surrender his staff and ring. Thereupon he laid his staff on the tomb of Edward the Confessor, saying, " Thou, O holy Edward, gavest me this staff, and to thee I restore it." Then turning to the Norman prelates and lords, he calmly said, " I received my staff from a better man than any of you, and to him I have returned it. Take it from him if you can." The impression produced on the council was so great that Wulstan was left in the undisturbed enjoyment of his bishopric. On his way back to his diocese his friends in Buckinghamshire received him with enthusiasm. They would doubtless be quite prepared to receive the story that was noised abroad, that Wulstan's staff had penetrated the stone of Edward's tomb, and lodged there so that no one could move it but Wulstan himself. For it was believed that Edward, among many other miracles, had restored to sight a Buckinghamshire man, Wulwin of Ludgershall; and had not Wulstan himself miraculously escaped from the falling house at Wycombe? Accordingly, he was asked to consecrate Wycombe parish church, which was then being built at the expense of a wealthy Saxon thane. Having obtained the consent of the Norman diocesan Remigius, Wulstan came and consecrated the church. Later tradition asserted that on this occasion he healed an afflicted girl with a piece of gold which had been touched by the Holy Lance (the spear which had pierced the Saviour's side); but unfortunately this was before the Holy Lance had been found at Antioch. On another occasion, the bishop visited Marlow. According to William of Malmesbury, in his *Vita Sancti Wulstani*, he found the roads in a frightful state, the weather having been very wet. The clergy who served the parish church were somewhat reluctant to turn out to matins in the cold, cheerless early morning. Wulstan, however, insisted on their coming with him. They led him round by the miriest road they could find, in order to force him to turn back, but the sturdy bishop trudged on through the mud, with the loss of one of his episcopal shoes. After saying matins in the church, he went back to breakfast, and then, without any expression of annoyance or complaint, quietly sent two priests in search of the missing shoe!

One more Buckinghamshire saint, of later date, but probably also of Saxon blood, may here be mentioned. Master John Shorne, or Schorne, rector of North Marston from 1290 till his death in 1314, was renowned far and near for his piety and his miraculous powers. It was believed that, like another St. James, he had caused his knees to become hard and horny by the frequency of his prayers. But more marvellous still, he was believed, when sore tempted by the Evil One, to have imprisoned the enemy in one of his boots! —" which astounding miracle raised him to the dignity of a saint, and won for him the veneration of centuries." Though he was never actually canonised, his shrine, which was removed in 1478 to St. George's Chapel, Windsor, became the resort of such multitudes that their offerings are said to have amounted to £500 per annum, representing fifteen or twenty times that amount in present values. There seems also to have been an image of him at Long Marston, much resorted to by pilgrims; and a well in the village, which still bears his name, and is remarkable for its purity and coldness, was said to have sprung up in answer to his prayers in time of drought.

Absurd as some of these legends now appear, there is one interesting point to be noted about them. The saints associated with and most honoured in Buckinghamshire were English saints—not, as in some counties, Celtic, or Roman, or Norman. Their stories point to a vigorous sense of Saxon nationality, which had not a little to do with preparing the way for the Lollard movement. Dr. Stoughton, in his *Church of the Civil Wars* (page 52), remarks that " the plain and sturdy nature of the Anglo-Saxon " always leaned to " a simple and unostentatious kind of religious worship," and was "unfriendly to that ecclesiastical pomp of architecture and glittering ritual which delighted the Norman." There is much truth in his further statement, that " traditional opinions and sentiments, opposed to the spirit of Romanism, had been handed down through the Middle Ages, from one generation to another of the English commonalty in their homesteads and cottages," and that " those opinions and sentiments contributed to the outbursts of Lollardism." Even where the Saxon accepted the teachings of the Roman Church, he gave them a colouring of his own.

CHAPTER II

THE ecclesiastical antiquities of this county are far less extensive and splendid than those of many others. Buckinghamshire never had any great abbey, like Glastonbury or St. Edmundsbury, nor any great collegiate foundation before Eton arose under Henry VI. Yet it was at Winslow, where, as at Brill and Cippenham, the kings of Mercia had a palace, that Offa planned the foundation of the mighty Abbey of St. Albans. Matthew Paris tells how a sudden light illuminated the oratory where bishops and priests, in response to the king's tearful entreaty, were seeking the Divine guidance, and how he resolved to endow the abbey with the royal manor of Winslow, which continued to belong to it until the Dissolution.

There are few remains of Saxon church architecture, beyond some stone-work at Iver, Wing, and Lavendon, and the tower of Caversfield church (formerly in Bucks, but now in Oxfordshire). Domesday Book shows very little land as belonging to the Church in this county, and mentions no religious house except one at North Crawley, founded under Edward the Confessor, and dedicated, like the parish church, to St. Firmin, Bishop of Amiens. It probably became extinct at an early date.

In Saxon times, Buckinghamshire was part of the diocese of Dorchester (Oxon). To this was afterwards annexed that of Sidnacester in Lincolnshire, when it became of enormous extent, reaching from the Thames to the Humber, and including seven archdeaconries. After the Norman Conquest, Remigius de Féchamp, "a dwarf in stature but a giant in soul," and a friend of the great Lanfranc, removed the see from Dorchester to Lincoln, to which diocese Bucks continued to belong till 1845.

Towards the close of the eleventh century, under William II., a Cluniac priory arose at Tickford, near Newport Pagnell, as a branch or "cell" of the great Abbey of Marmonstiers, or St. Martin, at Tours. This was one of the "alien priories," in which French monks came to reside, who collected the revenues, and transmitted them to the parent house. Not an unnatural arrangement when the English kings had possessions on the Continent, this became a very obnoxious one in later days, when war arose between England and France, and after many interferences on the part of the Crown, the alien priories were at last suppressed by Henry V.

Under Henry I. (1100-1135) a Benedictine or Cluniac priory appears to have been founded at Newton Longville, as a cell of the Abbey of St. Foy at Longueville in Normandy, by Walter

Giffard, Earl of Buckingham; while Robert
Bossu, Earl of Leicester, founded another Benedictine house at Luffield, in Whittlebury Forest,
and on the very borders of Northamptonshire.
The Abbey of St. Mary at Great Missenden is
said to have been founded by William de Missenden in 1133, for the black-robed and bearded
Austin Canons, "half monks, half secular
clergy;" but other authorities date it from 1293.

" At the close of Henry's reign," writes Mr.
J. R. Green (*History of the English People*, i.
156), " and throughout the reign of Stephen,
England was stirred by the first of those great
movements which it was to experience afterwards
in the preaching of the Friars, the Lollardism of
Wickliffe, the Reformation, the Puritan enthusiasm, and the mission work of the Wesleys.
Everywhere, in town and country, men banded
themselves together for prayer, hermits flocked
to the woods, noble and churl welcomed the aus-
tere Cistercians . . . . . A new spirit of devotion
woke the slumbers of the religious houses, and
penetrated alike to the home of the noble and the
trader." It was naturally to be expected that
many would seek retirement from the world
during the troubled days of Stephen (1135-1154).
And the Cistercians, the " White Monks of
Citeaux," whose rule bore the impress of the
sturdy English character of Stephen Harding, and
whose studied simplicity of life and worship was a
practical protest against the growing luxury and
worldliness of the degenerate Benedictines and

Cluniacs, were the very men to impress the time. A house of these monks, "the Quakers of the Middle Ages," was founded at Biddlesden in 1147 by Ernald de Bosco, steward to the Earl of Leicester, who dedicated it to St. Mary, and endowed it with his lands there "in wood and in plain." Another of the 115 monasteries built in England during Stephen's reign was an alien priory at Wing, a cell of the Abbey of St. Nicolas at Angers, which was founded in 1140, and was endowed with lands by the Empress Maud.

Under Henry II. (1154-1189) three Benedictine nunneries arose at uncertain dates. One, to which some attribute an earlier origin, was dedicated to St. Margaret, the virgin martyr of Antioch. It stood among the beech-crowned Chilterns, in a detached portion of the parish of Ivinghoe, upon the Herts border. Two more were on the banks of the Thames—St. Mary's at Little Marlow (called "the Priory of the Springs"), close to the present village of Well End; and St. Mary Magdalene's, Ankerwyke, at the extreme south of the county in the parish of Wraysbury. The Premonstratensians or White Canons had an abbey, dedicated to St. John the Baptist, at Lavendon, near Olney. In the beautiful vale of Notley, with its hazel-copses by the banks of the Thames, Walter Giffard, second Earl of Buckingham (son of the Earl who is said to have founded Newton Priory), and Ermentrude his wife, founded an Augustinian abbey, dedicated to the

Virgin and St. John the Baptist (1161), which
became very rich in lands and other possessions.
St. Mary's Priory at Bradwell, near Wolverton,
a Benedictine house, dated from about 1155 ; and
a small hospital at Ludgershall, a " cell " of an
abbey in Picardy, also had its origin in this reign.

The number of dedications to the Virgin is very
significant. One third of the ancient dedications
of parish churches in Buckinghamshire are also
to the " Blessed Virgin," or to her Nativity or
Assumption. This is said to have been largely
due to the influence of St. Hugh, Bishop of Lincoln 1186-1200, who earnestly promoted the cultus
which is thus indicated.

Under Richard I. (1189-1199) no religious
foundations are recorded in the county ; and under
John (1199-1216) only one. This was the small
Abbey of Medmenham, really a cell of the Cis-
tercian Abbey of Woburn, Beds, founded in 1201,
occupied by monks from Woburn in 1204, abandoned for a time, and then re-opened in 1212.

Early in the long reign of Henry III. (1216-
1272) we come to the foundation of the Benedictine Priory of Snelshall, on the borders of Whad-
don Chase (1218). In 1244 Sir Ralph de Norwich
(probably a veteran who had fought with Cœur
de Lion in Palestine) founded an Augustinian
priory at Chetwode ; and another sprang up at
Ravenstone in 1254, nominally originated by the
King, but really by Peter de Chaceport, the
keeper of his wardrobe. In 1265, the king's
brother Richard, King of the Romans, founded

an abbey for Benedictine nuns at Burnham, close to his manor-house at Cippenham.

Lastly, at an uncertain date in the reign of Edward I. (1272-1307), Edmund Earl of Cornwall, son of the Richard just mentioned, founded and munificently endowed a monastery or "College" for "Bonhommes" of the order of St. Augustine, at Ashridge, on the site now occupied by the palatial residence of Earl Brownlow. It became the most renowned place of pilgrimage in the county, for its founder presented it with a portion of the contents of a golden vessel, said to contain some of the blood of our Saviour, which he had obtained in Germany, and in honour of which he dedicated the College. The remainder he bestowed on an abbey founded by his father at Hales, in Gloucestershire. "The blood of Hales" is often mentioned in writings of the Reformation period. One account makes it the blood of a duck; but Henry VIII.'s commissioners declared it to be "an unctuous gum" coloured red. Mr. Pratt, in his notes on Foxe (vol. vii., p. 775), gives an extract from the *Liber Festivalis*, stating that it was not supposed to be the actual blood of Christ, but that of a miraculous crucifix, pierced by certain Jews. But Latimer, when living at West Kington, not far from Hales, says : "They believe verily that it was the very blood that was in Christ's body, shed upon the mount of Calvary for our salvation." The founder's heart was preserved at Ashridge in a golden shrine, along with that of St. Thomas de Cantilupe, Bishop of Hereford. A century later, Edward the Black Prince richly endowed the College of the Precious Blood, and presented it with a portion of the True Cross set in gold and gems.

This list of monasteries is not complete (e.g., there was certainly one at Aylesbury in early Norman times); but the rest were either very small, or soon fell into decay.

The monastic houses enjoyed curiously varied privileges. For example, Biddlesden, by a grant of Edward II., to whom the Abbot had lent money, had the right of holding a market every Monday, and an annual fair during six days. The nuns of Burnham, in the second year of Henry IV., acquired the right of holding a market and fair at Burnham, and a fair at Beaconsfield, the tolls of which were of course Abbey property, and also the right of claiming all goods confiscated for felony both in Burnham and Beaconsfield. The nuns of Marlow similarly held a fair at Ivinghoe. The Prior of Snelshall held weekly markets at Snelshall and Mursley. The Abbot of Notley held the advowson and tithes of several parishes, with exemption from payments in the county and hundred courts, freedom from market tolls throughout the realm, and the right to use two carts at certain seasons to bring wood from the royal forest of Bernwood. The nuns of Ankerwyke might feed sixty swine on the acorns of Windsor Forest. Strangest of all, the Prior of Tickford had the privilege of setting up a " pillory and tumbrill, to punish and chastise transgressors ;" while his near neighbour the Prior of Newton might keep his vassals in awe by means of his own private gallows.

A curious picture of a monastery farm is given in Dugdale's *Monasticon* (v. 205), in the shape of an inventory of the goods of Tickford Priory, early in the fourteenth century. There were 11 horses, 28 head of cattle, 54 sheep, 77 swine, 2 swans, 2 peacocks, 124 acres of wheat, 133 of oats, 15 of peas and vetches, 9 of bere (coarse barley), 4 of beans, and 3 of meadow-land, besides two acres "mixed." Each man-servant had the same allowance as a monk, but with an extra supply of bread and ale. Throughout England the monks were the best farmers. The sneer that

—" these black crows
Had pitched by instinct on the fattest pastures,"

loses its point when it is remembered that the sites they selected often owed their beauty and fertility to the patient toil of the brethren, having been at first unreclaimed wastes and swamps. The rule of the monks as landlords, too, was probably milder than that of the Norman baron, though we shall see that the great houses could be tyrannous enough to their tenants at times.

There were five leper houses in the county— two at Aylesbury, one at Wycombe, and one at Newport Pagnell (which still exists as an almshouse), and also a "chapel of

leprous women " at Bradley, belonging to
Notley Abbey. The inmates naturally lived a
semi-monastic life. Some have imagined that
leprosy was imported from the East by those
returning from the Crusades; but there are traces
of its existence in England at a much earlier date.
It was probably due to the general ignorance of
sanitary laws, and had greatly abated in virulence
by the close of the fourteenth century.

A more certain trace of the influence of the
Crusades is to be found in the fact that the two
great military orders of the Knights Templars
and Hospitallers held lands in various parts of
the county. The Templars would be well known
at Marlow, as they had a Preceptory at Bisham,
just across the river (where the name " Temple "
still survives); and the Hospitallers had a
Commandery at High Wycombe, the ruins of
which may still be seen in front of the Grammar
School, and another at Hogshaw, near Winslow.
Many a gallant Buckinghamshire knight doubtless
found his way to Palestine to fight against the
" misbelievers." Sir Ralph de Norwich has
already been referred to. John of Marlow, a
Knight Hospitaller, went with Prince Edward to
the last Crusade, and was slain at the siege of
Acre on Palm Sunday, 1270. Even in the early
part of the fifteenth century, John Cheyne, son
of the lord of Drayton Beauchamp, fought in
Palestine. And we may still see a reminder of
the Holy Wars in the " Saracen's Head," no
uncommon sign of Buckinghamshire inns.

CHAPTER III

IN estimating the religious condition of the
country before Lollardy arose, it is necessary to
take into account numerous elements, which
exercised a more wide-spread influence than the
monastic houses described in the last chapter.
These were scattered here and there; but in every
village there was a parish priest. There is reason,
however, to fear that these clergy were as a rule
sadly ignorant and inefficient. They preached
but little; and when Archbishop Peckham tried to
institute a reform in the days of Edward I., he
went no further than to require that every clerk
should deliver four sermons a year to his
parishioners!

The revenues of the Church were so largely
monopolised by the monasteries and the higher
ecclesiastics (many of the latter foreign nominees
of the Pope, and in some cases never entering
England) that the parish priests, like those of
Ireland at the present day, were largely dependent
on the dues and offerings of their people. In the
Records of Buckinghamshire (i. 233) a curious
document is cited, by which Bishop Sutton, in

1394, appoints Robert of Thame to " the newly
ordained vicarage of Bierton," with the duty of
holding service in the chapels of Bierton,
Quarrendon, Buckland, and Stoke. The revenues
of these four chapels are estimated at 36 marks
(£24), of course representing a far larger amount
at the present day. This included " all manner
of oblations, mortuaries, tithe of wool, lambs,
milk, flax, hemp, pigs, geese, eggs, foals of
horses, calves, gardens and crofts which are dug
with foot and spade, and also all the tithe of
pigeons," besides " certain corn, commonly called
Puttecorne, for the burial of the parishioners of
Hulcote, who are buried at Bierton." The parish
priest of Wycombe had " the tithe of teasels "
(used in fulling cloth).

The whole nation was nominally of one faith,
save for a handful of Jews. These were so few
that a law was passed under Henry II., restricting
their interments to one burying-ground near
London. In Buckinghamshire a few scattered in-
dividuals residing at Buckingham, Wycombe, and
Marlow, are all that have been traced by Jewish
antiquaries. In 1290, all Jews were expelled,
and the outward uniformity was complete.

The old Paganism, however, had died hard,
and traces of it were to be found at a much later
date than is commonly supposed. As late as the
reign of Henry II., St. Hugh, Bishop of Lincoln,
had complained that he found many relics of
heathenism in his diocese. (*Vita Sancti Hugonis*,
Rolls Series, 348). Amongst others, it is recorded

that he suppressed the worship of a certain "fountain" at Wycombe. This, it seems, was the spring at the east end of Wycombe Rye, by the piece of ground still known as Halliwell (Holy Well) Mead. But the worship of sacred springs was carried on, if in a modified form, for at least a century after the time of St. Hugh. In 1299 Bishop Sutton forbade the resort of pilgrims to the "holy well at Linslade," alleging that it had become a public scandal, and that the vicar had encouraged it for his own emolument.

Another Bishop of Lincoln, in the next century, had a deep and lasting influence throughout his vast diocese. Robert Grossetête, Bishop from 1235 to 1253, was born of humble peasant stock in Suffolk, and his whole career was not only that of a true Christian pastor, but that of a great English patriot. No "hireling that cared not for the sheep," no cold and unsympathising foreigner, he looked on each peasant and serf in his unwieldy diocese as a fellow-countryman and a brother in Christ. He has been styled "a Reformer before the Reformation," but his protests were against the corruptions of the Church in discipline, and the encroachments of the Papal Court, not against the received doctrines of Catholicism. He set himself against impropriation of tithes, against absentee and pluralist clergy, and against the holding of secular office by bishops and priests. He used all his influence to supply the parishes with suitable pastors, and refused to institute

incompetent men.   In his *Epistolæ*, published
in the Rolls Series, we find some allusions to
Buckinghamshire.   He protests against the appointment of the Abbot of Ramsey as itinerant
justice for the counties of Buckingham and
Bedford (p. 105).   He writes to the monks of
Missenden, who were about to elect an abbot,
and points out to them the responsible nature of
their choice, entreating them not to exercise less
care in the selection of a guardian of souls than
they would in that of one of their swineherds
(p. 268).   The suffrages of the monks fell upon
Roger of Aylesbury, and we must hope that he
realised the Bishop's ideal.

Grossetête regarded with favour the rise of a
new religious movement which characterised his
day—the work of the Friars, especially of the
Franciscans and Dominicans.   Through their
efforts, he said, " the people that sat in darkness
had seen a great light."   Indeed, the labours of
these men, who sought out the poor and degraded,
and preached with homely earnestness in street
and market-place, amounted to a religious revo-
lution, and tended to win back for the Church
much of the popular sympathy which had been
alienated by the aloofness of the monks and the
inefficiency of the parish priests.

The Dominicans or Black Friars first appeared
in England in 1221, the year of their founder's
death, when thirteen, landing at Dover, went
first to Oxford to convert the Jews, and then to
London.   Three years later, nine Franciscans or

Grey Friars landed penniless at Dover, and settled at Canterbury, at Oxford, and in " Stinking Lane by the Shambles at Newgate," henceforth known as Greyfriars. In thirty years their numbers in England had increased to over 1200. The Carmelites (White Friars) and Augustinians (Austin Friars) followed a few years later.

However warmly the Friars were received by the " common people," they were scarcely welcomed by the older Orders, whose comfortable devotion was disturbed by the ascetic life and noisy teaching of the new comers. The two first Grey Brothers who journeyed to Oxford lost their way in the woods between Oxford and Baldon (five or six miles from the Buckinghamshire border). Fearful of the floods, they sought shelter at a grange of the monks of Abingdon. " Their ragged clothes and foreign gestures, as they prayed for hospitality, led the porter to take them for jongleurs, the jesters and jugglers of the day, and the news of this break in the monotony of their lives brought prior, sacrist, and cellarer, to the door to welcome them and witness their tricks. The disappointment was too much for the temper of the monks, and the brothers were kicked roughly from the door to find their night's lodging under a tree."

No doubt the people of Buckinghamshire became familiar with the sight of Grey and Black Friars traversing the roads between Oxford and London. But it was not till 1368 that the Franciscans founded an establishment at Aylesbury, the only one of any order of Friars in the county; and the permanent Friary there was not built until some years later.

Although the preaching of the Friars was of course thoroughly Romanist (Wycliffe complains that they took for their texts the lives of the saints, and even popular tales and ballads, instead of the words of Scripture), and although they afterwards found means of evading their vow of poverty, acquired rich possessions, and were accused of greed, laziness, and licentiousness; still their work was of immense importance in preparing the way for the Lollard Reformation. Especially did they awaken a love of earnest, homely preaching which has largely characterised the English race ever since.

When we come to consider the traces of actual dissent from the teaching of the Church before the rise of Wycliffe, we find them singularly few and vague. Yet there was undoubtedly a good deal of secret dissent hidden below the surface; and it is curious that this is especially traceable in the adjoining county of Oxford. In 1166, according to William of Newburgh, a council was convened at Oxford to enquire into the heresy of a company of about thirty German weavers, called "Publicani," who had appeared in the diocese of Worcester. It is stated that Gerard, their leader, was a man of education, and that his answers showed him to be orthodox as to the person of Christ, but that he rejected baptism, marriage, the Eucharist, and the authority of the Church.

It is probably to be understood that he and his followers refused to accept the doctrine of sacramental grace, and held, like the Quakers, that marriage might be celebrated by mutual consent. Newburg states that Gerard and his followers, by the king's command, were stripped to the waist, scourged through the city of Oxford, and branded on the face with a hot iron. They sang as they endured their punishment, " Blessed shall ye be when men shall hate you." Then proclamation was made that all men were forbidden to give them food or shelter, and they were driven forth, with loud cracking of whips, to perish miserably of cold and hunger. Such is Newburgh's account; and if it is to be accepted, we might suppose that some of these unfortunate foreigners possibly met their fate among the hills and woods of Buckinghamshire. But Newburgh wrote long after, and in the north of England; and other chroniclers (Roger of Wendover, Walter Mapes, and Ralph of Coggeshall), say that the Publicani were banished from the realm after being scourged and branded.

The admission that these Publicani were orthodox as to the person of Christ is of importance as distinguishing them from the wilder heretical sects of the period. They probably held views similar to those of the Albigenses and Waldenses; and it is certain that Albigensian refugees found their way to England in the reign of John, when one was burned alive in London, and others in different parts of the country (Knyghton, col. 2418). Traces of the Waldenses are less distinct.

There is a reference in the *Custumale* of the
diocese of Rochester to certain tenants of the
manor of Darenth, settled there at some time between 1181 and 1197. These are described as
" Waldenses ;" but this may simply mean men
of the Walda, or Weald. Still more interesting
is an allusion in a document cited in Burn's *History of Henley* (p. 186). By a lease dated in the
6th of Henry IV., the Warden and Bridgemen of
Henley, demised to Master Edward Bekyn-
ham, rector of the Church of Henley,
a granary situate near the bridge, with a
chapel adjoining, " *quondam Waldeschenes.*"
Mr. Burn renders these last words, " formerly that
of the Waldenses," and goes so far as to suggest
that there may have been some connexion between
them and the followers of Gerard ! This certainly seems in the last degree unlikely ; and
indeed Mr. Burn seems to abandon the idea in a
later portion of his work (p. 237), on the ground
that the name of Waldense appears as a surname
in the Henley Court Rolls. Even this can hardly
be regarded, however, as decisive, when we remember the frequent significance of surnames in
the Middle Ages ; and it is at least curious that
Henley became a stronghold of Lollardy. Of
course if there were actually Waldenses, either at
Darenth or at Henley, they must have outwardly
conformed to the dominant Church ; but this was
the case with many of the Waldenses on the
Continent.

Under date of November 23rd, 1263, Foxe

(*Acts and Monuments*, ii. 559) gives a curious letter addressed by Henry III. to the Sheriff of Oxfordshire, requiring him to suppress " certain vagabond persons calling themselves Harloti," who were carrying on " meetings, conventicles, and unlawful contracts, against the honesty of the Church and of good manners." Foxe seems to think that this was a fanatical religious sect ; and the letter certainly seems to indicate some movement which had given alarm to the authorities of the Church.

So far we have found no trace of heresy in Buckinghamshire itself ; but the county, lying as it did between London with its love of freedom, and Oxford with its intellectual ferment and its multitudes of foreign students, was a district where " obstinate questionings " were likely to find an echo, as we shall see was actually the case.

CHAPTER IV

THE RECTOR OF LUDGERSHALL

THE reign of Edward III. is one of the most significant epochs in our English history. It was characterised by the final blending into one national life of the Saxon and Norman elements, and by the recognition of English as the national language; by the birth of English literature in Chaucer and Langland; and by the first stirring of agrarian and democratic movements, which have told on the whole of our subsequent history.

This great formative period was the real birth-time of the English Reformation. Protestantism in England was not the offspring of the caprice of Henry VIII. Kings can do but little towards changing the faith of the classes in which the real strength of a country's religion lies. The Reformation of the sixteenth century was the inevitable resultant of a series of forces which had been at work for ages, and which had found an embodiment a century and a half before in the life and teachings of John Wycliffe, for six years the rector of a Buckinghamshire parish.

The estimate of John Wycliffe's greatness has steadily increased with the lapse of time. Here

and there some obscure writer may affect to
believe that his splendid career of opposition to
the Papacy finds its explanation in spite, at being
deprived of a wardenship at Oxford; though it
is very doubtful whether the John Wycliffe or
Wyclyve who was Warden of Canterbury Hall,
by the appointment of Archbishop Islip, and who
was dispossessed in 1367 by Archbishop Langham,
was not quite another person, the parish priest
of Mayfield in Sussex. Anyhow, it is certain that
Islip was at Mayfield at the time of the appointment, having been seized with an attack of
paralysis while on a journey.

Continental scholars, like Lechler and Loserth,
with a truer appreciation of Wycliffe's greatness
than that shown by some of his countrymen, have
seen in him the master-mind, not only of the
English, but of the European Reformation.
Milton was not so far wrong when he wrote in
his *Areopagitica*, " Had it not been for the
perverseness of our prelates, against the divine
and admirable Wicklef, to suppress him as a
schismatic and innovator, perhaps neither the
Bohemian Huss and Jerome, no, nor the name
of Luther or of Calvin, had ever been known. The
glory of reforming all our neighbours had been
completely ours."

Born near Wycliffe-on-Tees, in the extreme
north of Yorkshire, about 1320, Wycliffe pursued
his studies at Oxford with such success that in
or about 1360 he became Master of Balliol. In
1361 he was presented by that College to the living

of Fillingham in Lincolnshire. He still continued, however, to reside mainly at Oxford, probably providing a curate to supply his place at Fillingham.

In 1368, Wycliffe obtained two years' leave of absence from Fillingham, and the same year he exchanged the living for the less valuable rectory of Ludgershall, in Buckinghamshire, so as to be nearer Oxford.

Ludgershall is a tiny village, about 12 miles N.E. of Oxford, and nearly the same distance W.N.W. of Aylesbury. The old church, with an embattled tower, stands at the top of a sloping village green. The scenery around is somewhat flat, except to the south, where the picturesque heights of Brill and Ashendon divide the plain of North Bucks from the Vale of Aylesbury. Over the south porch of the church was formerly a parvise, or priest's chamber, the spiral stair leading to which from the aisle may still be traced. This chamber seems to have been destroyed in a restoration a few years ago, a loss which is to be regretted, because the parvise was often used as a study, and a doubtful tradition has it that here Wycliffe wrote his great work, *De Civili Dominio*.

The village was probably a place of greater relative importance then than now. The Roman Akeman Street, and the broad trackway from Oxford to Cambridge, passed through the parish. The Knights of St. John had presented Wycliffe to the living. Their office was to protect travellers, and they had a hospice at Ludgershall, just on the borders of Bernwood Forest. There was also, as we have seen, a small " alien priory."

It is not easy for us to picture the conditions of life in a village like Ludgershall in the fourteenth century. Many of Wycliffe's parishioners would be serfs and villeins, almost as much a part of the estate they tilled as the cattle or the trees ; clad in the coarsest garments, living on the poorest food, and inhabiting wattled hovels, with smoke-holes instead of chimneys. The winter floods are troublesome at Ludgershall even now, but would be far worse then. The old people would remember the Seven Years' Famine (1315—1321), the most terrible in English history. And worst of all, twenty years before Wycliffe came to the village (1348), the Black Death, after slaying its tens of millions both in Asia and Europe, had made its appearance in Dorsetshire, and crept slowly northward and eastward. The grass grew in the streets of Bristol. The lads who were crowded together, living on the barest fare, in the hostels of Oxford, died by hundreds after a few hours' sickness. Fifty thousand corpses were interred in one great burying-ground outside the gates of London. In the country, cattle roamed about ownerless, and the harvests rotted in the fields. At Winslow, ten miles from Ludgershall, 153 holdings changed hands in a few months, and 37 out of 43 jurymen of the manor court died. A milder outbreak marked the year 1361, while Wycliffe was Master of Balliol. A

third came in 1368, just after his settlement at
Ludgershall, and the fourth and last in 1375.

Some writers have maintained that Wycliffe
held the living of Leckhamstead, near Buckingham, at the same time as that of Ludgershall.
In the will of William de Askeby, Archdeacon
of Northampton, made just before his death in
1371, and preserved in the Lambeth Register, is
a legacy of " 100s. or one best robe " to " John
de Wyclif, rector of Lekehamstede." The
principal executor of this will is " John de Wyclif,
rector of Ludgershale." Hence some have
thought that the rector of Leckhamstead was a
kinsman of the Reformer. But John de Barton
was rector there from 1361 to 1365, when he resigned, and was followed by John D'Autre.
Moreover, there is a tick in the margin of the
Register against " Lekehamstede," as if to hint
at some error. Possibly the dying Archdeacon
dictated the word by a momentary inadvertence
or failure of memory. Wycliffe could hardly
have protested as strongly as he did against
pluralists, if it had been known that he was a
pluralist himself.

Some very vague traditions are preserved in a
part of the county rather remote from Ludgershall, which have to do with Wycliffe. In the
little town of Colnbrook, through which he would
probably pass on his journeys between Oxford and
London, a family named Weekly used to claim
a descent from him, which if true, must have
been of course a collateral one. Close by, at

Longford, in Middlesex, an old house was long
pointed out as having given him shelter in some
time of danger; and not very far off is the Crouch
Oak at Addlestone, in Surrey, under which a
very doubtful tradition states that he preached.

Roughly speaking, Wycliffe's life-work may be
divided into three periods—academic, political,
and spiritual.   It was during the second that he
was rector of Ludgershall.   England was asserting its independence of the Papal Court at
Avignon, the influence of which had been lessened
by Edward III.'s French victories.   The
Statutes of Provisors and Præmunire (1350, 1353)
had challenged the Pope's right to interfere in
English affairs.   In 1366, however, Urban V.
unwisely required the King to pay the tribute
promised by John, with thirty years' arrears, or
else to appear before him as his feudal superior,
and answer for his neglect.   The spirit of the
nation was thoroughly roused.   There was a
growing intolerance of priestly pretensions, a
significant instance occurring in Buckinghamshire two or three years before this, when the
Abbot of Missenden, who had been convicted
of illegal coining, was sentenced to be hanged,
drawn, and quartered, a doom he escaped by
means of the Royal pardon.   Parliament repudiated the Papal claim, and declared John's surrender of the Crown null and void.   Further
anti-Papal legislation followed (1371 to 1374);
and in the latter year the now aged King
appointed a Commission to treat with Papal

delegates at Bruges on the points at issue between England and the Pope. There were seven commissioners, and Wycliffe's name stands second on the list. The negotiations proved to a large extent fruitless, but Edward showed his appreciation of Wycliffe's services by offering him on his return a prebendal stall in Worcester Cathedral, which he declined. Earlier in the year, however, he had accepted the living of Lutterworth in Leicestershire, on which appointment he seems to have immediately resigned the living of Ludgershall. The ties which bound him to Oxford had been weakened (if he was indeed the dispossessed Warden of Canterbury Hall) by the action of Archbishop Langham ; and he no longer felt the need of a residence near the University. Henceforth he was to speak not so much to scholars as to the English nation at large.

Lechler (page 367) thinks that it was not until after the Papal Schism (1378) that Wycliffe began to send out his famous itinerant preachers, the " Poor Priests," and that Lutterworth was the headquarters of the mission. His translator, Dr. Lorimer, however (page 201, note) says :—
" The prevalence of Lollard doctrines in after years throughout the districts lying immediately to the east of Oxfordshire seems to point to some original centre of activity in that neighbourhood ; and as Wycliffe held the living of Ludgershall from 1368 till 1374, the probability seems to be that the plan was originated there." Lechler's suggested date certainly seems too late, in view

of the proportions which the movement had
reached at the date of the " Earthquake Council "
in 1382.   But the Lollard districts in this part
of the country group themselves far more naturally
round Oxford itself than round Ludgershall; for
as we shall see, while we meet with hundreds of
instances in South Bucks, which lies between
Oxford and London, but is cut off from Ludgershall by the Chiltern Hills, there is scarcely one
recorded for the north of the county.   There are,
on the other hand, numerous cases in the parts
of Oxfordshire and Berkshire which lie to the
west and south of the University City.

Wycliffe's preachers do not all seem to have
been in orders; and towards the end of his life
he speaks of them as " evangelical men," rather
than as " priests."   Clad in russet gowns, with
bare feet, they travelled with staff is hand from
town to town, preaching in the churches when
allowed, or otherwise in the churchyard, street,
or market-place, like Wesley's itinerants four
centuries later.

Though Wycliffe had in him something of the
typical Conservatism of the college don, it was
curiously mingled with broad popular sympathies,
and he was perhaps the first to see the importance
of influencing the common people, and especially
those of the country districts, in the direction of
religious reform.   Speaking of Christ, he says :—
" The Gospel relates how He went about in the
places of the country, both great and small, in
cities and castles, or in the small towns ; and

this He did that He might teach us how to be
profitable to men generally, and not to forbear to
preach to the people because they are few, and
our name may not in consequence be great.
For we should labour for God, and from Him
hope for our reward.   There is no doubt that
Christ went into such small uplandish towns as
Bethphage and Cana of Galilee; for Christ went
to all those places where He wished to do good.
He was not smitten either with pride or covetous-
ness " (*Tracts and Treatises*, 85).

It was by men imbued with this spirit that the
doctrines of Wycliffe were spread in the " uplandish towns " and villages of the south of
Buckinghamshire.   These doctrines shaped themselves more clearly towards the close of his life;
and although they were not such as to prevent his
remaining a priest of the Catholic Church, they
held within them the germs of far-reaching
change.   He taught the right of private judgment,
the sole and sufficient authority of Scripture as a
rule of faith, and the direct responsibility of each
soul to God.   The ministry was necessary to the
well-being of the Church, but not to its existence,
and the logical outcome of his teaching pointed
both to Voluntaryism and to Presbyterian govern-
ment.   The Pope was Antichrist, and his cen-
sures were not to be feared.   Wycliffe repudiated
baptismal regeneration and transubstantiation,
but taught a doctrine of the presence of Christ
in the Eucharist somewhat resembling the later
consubstantiation of Luther.   But the view which

perhaps attracted most attention in his own time,
and was most keenly controverted, was his doctrine of " dominion founded in grace." God, as
the great feudal Superior of the Universe, had not,
he said, granted dominion to one man as His Vicar
on earth. The King was as much God's Vicar
as the Pope, and indeed every Christian held his
rights immediately of God.

We can only briefly refer to the subsequent
portion of Wycliffe's life. Summoned before the
Convocation of Canterbury at St. Paul's Cathedral, he was protected by the intervention of John
of Gaunt; and when in the following year he had
to appear before the Archbishop at Lambeth, Sir
Lewis Clifford, a gentleman of the household of
the Princess Joan, mother of the young King
Richard II., appeared to stay further proceedings
in her name.

Wycliffe continued at times to give divinity
lectures at Oxford after settling at Lutterworth.
Perhaps he may now and again have visited his
old flock at Ludgershall, and no doubt would take
care that his preachers visited the district. But
now (1381) the University condemned his views
on the Eucharist; John of Gaunt withdrew his
patronage; and in the same year an event took
place which proved a great injury to his cause,
though it would be an exaggeration to say with
Green that " in a few months the whole of his
work was undone."

The depopulation of the country by the Black
Death had deranged the whole relations between

capital and labour. The authorities had blindly
sought to stay the social changes which were
taking place by harsh and oppressive statutes
regulating the rate of wages and the price of food.
At last, maddened by the imposition of a poll-tax,
the peasantry rose over half the country. Wat
Tyler marched on London with the men of Kent
and Essex. The tenants of the great abbeys—
Glastonbury, St. Albans, Beverley, Bury St.
Edmunds—were especially embittered against
their mitred lords, and not without cause, if we
may judge by the conduct of the St. Albans
authorities towards their tenants in the Buckinghamshire parishes of Winslow, Grandborough,
Aston Abbots, and Little Horwood. " Instances
are not wanting," says Mr. A. Clear in his
History of the Town and Manor of Winslow, " in
which the lord " (i.e., the Abbot) " to show his
authority, issued the most trivial orders, such as
directing that the tenants should go off to the
woods and pick nuts for his use. If the ' Nativi '
married without the lord's consent, they were
fined ; if they allowed their houses to get out of
repair, they were fined for being guilty of waste ;
if they sold an ox without the license of the lord,
again they were fined ; if they left the manor
without permission, they were searched for, and
if found, arrested and brought back into servitude.
. . . . In all these offences, the whole of the jury
were also fined if they neglected to report the
delinquent." The tenants were obliged to plough
the Abbot's land for so many days in the year,

to cut his hay and corn, and perform various kinds of servile work. If they showed any tendency to insubordination, their horses and cattle were confiscated, and they were cast into prison. But the grievance which seems to have been most bitterly resented was the obligation to grind their corn at the Abbot's mill, and to pay for its use. The handmills in their houses were confiscated and turned into paving-stones for the abbey cloisters. When the news reached the Buckinghamshire manors of the rising of the citizens of St. Albans, under the spirited leadership of William Grindecobbe, the peasants hastened to the help of their Hertfordshire brethren. They tore up the millstones, carried them home in triumph, and extorted from the terrified monks ("by force and sheer roguery," as the latter declared) "charters such as were never before held by bondmen." But the insurrection was soon quelled; Grindecobbe paid the penalty of his boldness with his life, and the charters were declared null and void.

Wycliffe's opponents declared, and the allegation has been repeated ever since, that the commons had been incited to rebellion by his poor priests. If they sympathised with the sufferings of the peasantry, it was very much to their credit. But certainly if they shared the views of their great leader, these were very far from giving sanction to any such violent proceedings as those which characterised the revolt. It is true that John Ball, "the mad priest of

Kent," was said to have confessed himself a follower of Wycliffe. But such confessions, in those days of torture, signify very little ; and Ball had been accused of " many errors and scandals " fifteen years before. He was probably older than Wycliffe, and Knyghton calls him the latter's " precursor," not his follower.

The insurgents did Wycliffe great disservice, not only by bringing discredit on the movement he had originated, but by murdering the gentle and lenient Archbishop Sudbury, whom by the way, they accused of discouraging pilgrimages to Canterbury, which does not look much as if they were Wycliffites. His death made way for the promotion to the Primacy of Wycliffe's bitterest antagonist, William Courtenay, Bishop of London. Courtenay assembled a synod to condemn the doctrines of Wycliffe. It met at the Blackfriars Monastery in London on May 21st, 1382, and was known as the " Earthquake Council," from the fact that the City was shaken by an earthquake during the proceedings. But neither Courtenay nor any other of his foes ventured to lay hands on Wycliffe, and he remained in peaceable possession of his living at Lutterworth till his death on the last day of the year 1384.

CHAPTER V

THE EARLY DAYS OF LOLLARDY

THE name "Lollard," as applied to the followers of Wycliffe, is first met with in the latter years of the Reformer's life (about 1382). It had previously been applied to "heretics" who had arisen in Germany and other parts of the Continent, even as far east as Livonia. The origin of the word is much disputed. It seems at the time to have been connected with the word *lolium*, "tares;" and Walden calls Wycliffe's doctrines "bundles of tares." But the etymologies of that time are notoriously fanciful. Nor is there any ground for the idea that the name was derived from that of a German heretic called Lolhard. The word "loll," to lounge, has been suggested; but a more likely derivation is from the German word *lollen*, to sing softly (with which our words "lull" and "lullaby" are connected). The fact that the Lollards never seem to have been addicted to psalm-singing has been cited as an argument against this derivation; but the word may have been intended to satirise some alleged peculiarity of tone, and used with some of the vague significance of the modern word

" ranter." In the *Political Songs Poems and Songs* (Rolls Series, ii. 244), occur the lines :—

> And pardé, lolle thei never so longe,
> Yut wull lawe make hem lowte (i.e., Yet
> will law make them submit).

The Archbishop obtained from the young king after the Earthquake Council a royal ordinance for the arrest and imprisonment of the itinerant preachers. Strangely enough, this was entered as an Act of Parliament, though the Commons had never consented to its passing, and afterwards vainly demanded its repeal. It was, however, by no means easy to put the so-called Statute in force. The Lollards had many powerful supporters among knights and noblemen ; and Henry of Knyghton asserts that some of these were accustomed to summon their tenants to listen to the preaching of the " poor priests," and to stand beside the preacher armed with sword and shield for his defence.

Were any of these militant supporters of Lollardy to be found in Buckinghamshire? A paper in the *Archæologia* (ix. 375) says of John de Montacute, nephew of the Earl of Salisbury, " He was one of the chief of the sect called Lollards, and the greatest fanatic of them all, being so transported with zeal, that he caused all the images that were in. the chapel at Schenele (Shenley in Buckinghamshire), that had been set up there by the ancestors of his wife, to be taken down and thrown into obscure places; only the image of St. Catherine, in regard that many did affect it, he gave leave that it should stand in his bakehouse." The writer is in error as to the locality. The Shenley referred to was not that in Buckinghamshire, but Shenley in Hertfordshire, between Barnet and St. Alban's, where Montacute had lands in right of his wife. As to this "fanatic," he was in reality one of the most scholarly and accomplished men of his time. A French chronicler, the Monk of St. Denys, instead of heaping on him opprobrious epithets such as are bestowed upon him by Lancastrian scribes like Walsingham and Knyghton, calls him "humble, gentle, and courteous in all his doings," "loyal and chivalrous in all places," "bold and courageous as a lion;" and adds, "so gracious were all his deeds, that never, I think, shall that man issue from his country, in whom God has implanted so much goodness as was in him." At a later period, by his uncle's death, Montacute became possessed of Bucks manors at Datchet and Aston Clinton. Another manor in the latter parish belonged to Sir Philip de la Vache, K.G., who sat for Bucks as knight of the shire in 1386, and who also held the estate of the Vache at Chalfont St. Giles. Sir Philip married a daughter of the Lollard leader, Sir. Lewis Clifford, already referred to; and it has been suggested that he was probably inclined to Lollardy himself. At Aston Clinton he would be a near neighbour of the well-known Cheyne family of Drayton Beauchamp, as well as of Chesham Bois and Chenies, which were near his other estate of Chalfont. Thomas Cheyne, a member of this family, and a personal attendant of Richard II., was imprisoned in the Tower for rebellion and heresy a few years later. We thus see that there existed in South Bucks a little circle of landed proprietors, who would be more or less certainly in favour of the movement; and as a matter of fact we shall find that the district lying round Chalfont and Chesham was the very part where the principles of Lollardy took their deepest root.

In or about 1388 there appeared a revision of Wycliffe's translation of the Scriptures, supposed to have been from the hands of his friend John Purvey. Of this, 150 copies of the whole or part are still extant, a truly remarkable number considering the attempts made to suppress it, over and above the ordinary ravages of time. It evidently had a wide circulation, of course in MS.

In 1395, a memorial was presented to Parliament by Sir Thomas Latimer and Sir Richard Story, which set forth in " Twelve Conclusions " the reforms demanded by the Lollards. Their sweeping character marked an advance on the views of Wycliffe. Church endowments, vows of celibacy, transubstantiation, the exorcism and benediction of inanimate objects, the holding of secular office by the clergy, prayers for the dead, pilgrimages, image-worship, and auricular confession, were alike denounced, as well as war, capital punishment, and the practice of unnecessary arts. Great excitement followed, and King Richard, who was in Ireland, returned to England and summoned before him Montacute, Clifford, Latimer, Story, and others. His attitude towards the movement had previously been somewhat favourable, but he now gave the Lollards clearly to understand that they must look for no support from him. Still, persecution did not become very acute during his reign. In 1399, however, he was dethroned, and the crown was seized by his cousin Henry of Lancaster. The new King at once ordered the prelates to take measures for the suppression of heresy, and the arrest of the wandering preachers. At the Christmas of 1399, John de Montacute, now Earl of Salisbury, with some other nobles, attempted to seize Henry at Windsor Castle, and restore Richard. The plot failed, and after a skirmish at Maidenhead Bridge, the conspirators fled to the west, and were seized and beheaded at Cirencester. The Monk of St. Denys, who was in England at the time, says that the heads of the Lollard Earl and seven of his companions, borne aloft on spear-points, were brought into London to the sound of trumpets, and were met by the Bishop and clergy in their robes, chanting the *Te Deum*.

The murder of the fallen king probably took place in 1400; but for years many refused to believe in his death. In 1401, as recorded in the *Archæologia* (xxiii. 135), Henry was informed by one of the Grey Friars of Aylesbury that a priest attached to the Friary had expressed his pleasure at hearing a report that Richard was still alive.   Henry sent for him, and asked if this were true.

"I am glad," answered the priest, "as a man is glad of the life of his friend ; for I am beholden to him, and all my kin ; for he was our furtherer and promoter."

"With which would you hold," asked Henry, "if you saw me and King Richard fighting?"

"Forsooth, with him," said the brave priest ; "for I am more beholden to him."

"What would you succour him with?" asked the King, sneeringly.

"With a staff, perhaps," was the undaunted reply.

"What would you do with me, then?"

"I would make you Duke of Lancaster."

"Ah," said the tyrant, "thou art no friend of mine ; and thou shalt lose thine head."

No doubt many of the Lollard neighbours of this outspoken cleric shared his feelings, for they soon had cause to look back regretfully to the gentler days of Richard.   In 1400, as recorded in Wilkins' *Concilia* (ii ; 248) one John Seynon, " of Dounton in the diocese of Lincoln," recanted Lollard doctrines.   He may have been of Dunton near Winslow, though perhaps more probably of Dunton Basset near Lutterworth.   In 1401, the Court Rolls of the manor of Wycombe contain the entry, "Item, they present that John Dryvere doth not set up a cross upon his house."

The Lollards, we are told, held that "all they who do worship and reverence the sign of the cross do commit idolatry;" and whether Dryvere was a Lollard or not, it seems likely that the authorities wished to show their zeal for orthodoxy by calling attention to his omission.

This year (1401) was marked by the enactment of the terrible statute *De Hæretico Comburendo*, by which obstinate or lapsed heretics were liable to be publicly burned to death. William Sawtre, a priest from Lynn, suffered in London this year as the proto-martyr of Lollardy.

The new law was met in some quarters with a burst of indignation. It would almost seem from the Patent Rolls (2 Hen. IV. iv. 17) that the Friars, who were regarded as instigators of the measure, could hardly pass through the streets of Oxford or Cambridge without having their habits torn from their shoulders by the students. But the Statute had a crushing effect on the Lollards as a body. Among others, Sir Lewis Clifford, now nearly eighty years of age, abjured their doctrines. The terms of his will, " probably the result of mental and bodily infirmity," express the most abject contrition for his heresy, and he styles himself "false and traitor to his Lord God." He bequeaths certain Catholic devotional books to his daughter, the wife of Sir Philip de la Vache. As Sir Philip was in high favour with the new king, he also must have renounced Lollardy, if he had ever embraced it.

Although continual efforts were made to stamp

out Lollardy throughout the reign of Henry IV.,
the work of repression was far from being entirely
successful.   There were still persons of influence
who sheltered the wandering evangelists; and
there was a strong tendency even among the
orthodox laity to withstand the encroachments
of the clergy.   In 1410 the Commons petitioned
the Crown to resume the superfluous revenues of
the Church.   These they estimated as being

> As much as would maintain to the King's
> honour
> Full fifteen earls and fifteen hundred knights,
> Six thousand and two hundred good esquires,
>
> .   .   .   .
>
> A hundred almshouses right well supplied,
> And to the coffers of the King beside
> A thousand pounds by the year.

Such is Shakespeare's account (*Henry V.*, Act
i., Scene i.); but the actual sum named by the
Commons appears to have been far larger.   This
daring proposal is ascribed by Spelman in his
History of Sacrilege to a Buckinghamshire knight,
Sir John Cheyne, one of the Lollard family
already referred to.   The Commons also petitioned
for the relaxation of the Statute of Heretics; but
neither request was granted.

CHAPTER VI

THE FALL OF THE OLDER LOLLARDY

THE death of Henry IV., in 1413, and the accession of his son as Henry V., were followed by the initiation of far more stringent measures against the Lollards. Sir John Oldcastle, a personal friend of the young King, and one of the most distinguished soldiers of the time, was charged with heresy, and summoned to appear before the Archbishop of Canterbury. He at first refused to do so; but on the King intervening, he surrendered himself. On his refusal to abjure, he was excommunicated, and handed over to the secular power to be burned; but before the sentence could be carried into effect, he fled from the Tower, and remained for some time concealed in or near the borders of Wales, where his ancestral estates were situated.

Three or four months after this event, it was suddenly given out that 20,000 Lollards were marching on London from the country, and that a much larger number, mostly servants and apprentices, were ready to throw open the City gates and join them. The gates were held by a strong force of troops; all egress was forbidden; and the young king rode in from Eltham, raised the standard of the cross as in a solemn crusade, and rode out with his men-at-arms on Sunday evening, January 7th, 1414, to St. Giles's Fields. Here he found a large body of people, who are described as on horseback, but appear to have been unarmed. Numerous arrests were made, not only at " Thicket Field," in St. Giles's, but at Harringay, near Hornsey, and within the City itself. Five days later, thirty-nine persons were hanged and burned in St. Giles's Fields, after a hasty trial. The chroniclers name Sir Roger Acton, William Murle, a rich brewer of Dunstable, John Beverley, a preacher, and John Brown.

What was the object of this gathering? It was asserted that the Lollards intended to kill the King and his three brothers, with all the prelates and nobles, to rase to the ground all the cathedrals and abbeys, and to compel all monks and friars to earn their living. On the other hand, most Protestant writers have followed Foxe in his contention that the gathering in St. Giles's Fields was nothing but a religious assembly to listen to the preaching of Beverley. It seems most likely that the Lollards had formed some wild plan of revolt. Many of them, no doubt, regarded the rule of the House of Lancaster as a usurpation. Then, too, if there is any truth in Shakespeare's portraiture of " Mad Prince Hal," and if, as is stated, the Lollards had deduced from Wycliffe's doctrine of " dominion founded in grace " the dangerous corollary that a wicked

ruler had forfeited his right to rule, the King's
early life may have seemed to the Lollards to
justify an insurrection, in which they may have
hoped to be supplied with arms by their friends
within the City. May not the movement, really
have been (like the risings in 1402 and 1405, and
the Earl of Cambridge's plot in 1415), in favour
of young Edmund Mortimer, whose pretensions
it was not safe to name publicly, as he was in
the power of King Henry at the time? It is at
least suggestive that places in Herefordshire
pointed out as refuges of the Lollards, including
the curious little building in Deerfold Forest,
traditionally known as the "Lollard Chapel,"
are close to the old stronghold of the Mortimers
at Wigmore. Oldcastle himself is said to have
believed that Richard II. was still alive in Scotland; and it is surely just as likely that the
movement was really a Legitimist one as that
it had the levelling and Socialistic character
ascribed to it by some writers.

In the Patent Rolls of Henry V. we find a
document (1 Hen. V. v. 24) setting forth that
William Turnour, Walter Yonge, and John
Hazelwode, of Agmondesham (Amersham) and
John Fynche, of Missenden, had been sentenced
to death for favouring certain "preachers against
the King's person," and their goods and chattels
confiscated to the Crown; further, that the King,
compassionating their widows, Isabel Turnour,
Alice Yonge, Isabel Hazelwode, and Matilda
Fynche, granted the said goods and chattels to

them for the support of themselves and children.
It does not appear whether these four men, evidently in a respectable position in life, had been
executed in Buckinghamshire, or whether, as is
more probable, they were among those put to
death in St. Giles's Fields. Turner and Finch
are still common names in the district.

A little later (Pat. 2 Hen. V. ii. 1; iii. 23) we
find the King pardoning certain persons who had
been sentenced to be hanged, drawn, and quartered, for their complicity in the alleged rebellion.
Among those in the first list, numbering twenty-
seven, appear the names of John Angret, parson
of Isenhamstead Latimer, who had been presented to the living by Richard II. in 1396; Thomas
Sydyly, *alias* Sedely, of Wycombe Heath,
fletcher; and aso one Horton, *alias* Spycer, late
of Wycombe, but now of Coffin Lane, Dowgate
Ward, cooper. Another name is that of John
Wytheryn, parson of the church of Wydyngton,
perhaps Wiggenton, a parish in Herts, but almost
surrounded by Buckinghamshire. At the head of
the second list stands the name of John Langacre
of Wycombe, formerly of London; and the fourth
name (there are thirteen in all) is that of Richard
Sprotford, of Agmondesham, carpenter. Out of
forty names in these two lists, there are thus five
belonging to Buckinghamshire. There appear to
be two from London, four from Oxfordshire (one
a student, and one a parish priest) five from
Northamptonshire, five from Leicestershire, two
from Yorkshire, and one from each of the counties

of Warwick, Suffolk, Lincoln, Bedford, Derby, Chester, Essex, and Somerset. Of the remaining eight, one or two are illegible, and in the rest the county is not stated. It will be noted that the counties most numerously represented are just those the road from which would enter London by St. Giles, and that the band would pass through Buckinghamshire at the time when it had probably swollen to formidable numbers, and would thus encourage local sympathisers to join it. Five out of the forty were priests. Oldcastle himself is said to have been near London, to have had a narrow escape from arrest somewhere close to St. Albans, and to have fled again into Wales; but the accounts are vague and confused.

So far we have traced nine persons in Buckinghamshire (including one who had removed to London) as having been concerned in the movement; and all of these belong to the district round Wycombe and Amersham. Local tradition tells of a Lollard who is said to have been put into a barrel lined with tenter-hooks, and rolled down a steep field to the north of Amersham Church. Hence, it is said, the name of " Tenter Field "[1] which it still bears. On the opposite side of the town, close to the Upper Baptist Chapel (an ancient Nonconformist meeting-house to which we shall have occasion to refer again) is a meadow known as Harbour Field. Here, till a few years ago, was a clump of aged trees, wych-elm and sycamore, pointed out by a vague tradition as a

[1] See note, p. 54.

favourite resort of the Lollards. I once heard at
Amersham a curious story, the source of which I
have entirely forgotten, concerning a Lollard who
had climbed among the thick boughs of one of
these trees to read a MS. book, when the precious
scroll slipped from his grasp, fluttered to the
ground, and led to his arrest. We cannot attach
much importance to these vague legends, and the
story of the barrel of tenter-hooks seems particu-
larly improbable.[1] If ever such an atrocity was
committed, it would probably be in some outbreak
of popular violence, such as might be expected to
follow the suppression of the revolt of 1414. In
any case, the Nonconformists of the neighbourhood, with a true instinct, have never ceased to
regard their Lollard forefathers as the first
pioneers in the struggle for religious and civil
liberties, which was so nobly carried on upon the
same spot by their Quaker and Puritan successors
of the seventeenth century.

But the nine already named were not the only
or the most important Buckinghamshire men
charged with complicity in the rising. In
Rymer's *Foedera* (ix. 120) is preserved a document in which a general pardon is granted to the
Lollards, with certain exceptions. Among those
excepted are Sir John Oldcastle, Sir Thomas

---

[1] Further, the name " Tenter Field " is common in old maps
of the 17th century, and earlier, (*e.g.* Ogilby and Morgan's
Map of London, 1677) as the name of fields where cloth is
stretched on " tenters " (frames fitted with tenter-hooks) to
dry.

Talbot, Thomas Cheyne, the younger son of Roger
Cheyne, lord of Drayton Beauchamp, and Thomas
Drayton, rector of the some parish, both of the
last being prisoners in the Tower.   Thomas
Cheyne seems to have made his submission, as
he was at liberty shortly afterwards.   Browne
Willis says that Roger Cheyne himself died and
was buried in the Tower about this time; but
this seems doubtful, as a memorial slab, believed
to be his, exists in the parish church of Cassing-
ton, Oxfordshire, where the Cheynes had an
estate.   It is not a little remarkable, however,
that there exists an inquisition of his extensive
property in the counties of Buckingham, Oxford,
and Herts, which seems to have been made during
his lifetime, as though his estates had been forfeited by some offence.   If so, they were restored
to his elder son John, who was several times
Knight of the Shire and Sheriff of Bucks.   John
Cheyne, like his younger brother, displayed
earnest religious zeal, although in an opposite
direction.   He made a pilgrimage to the Holy
Land, and received the honour of knighthood for
his exploits there.   His epitaph states that he
endured great hardships among the Saracens, that
he slew a giant near the Holy Sepulchre, and
that he lived fifty-five years after his return, and
reached the age of nearly a hundred.   A few
years ago the grave of this Sir John Cheyne was
opened, when it was discovered that he must have
been nearly seven feet in height, and that his
teeth were sound and perfect to the last.   After

the death of his widow, who survived him twenty-
six years, the manor of Drayton passed to his
great-nephew, John Cheyne of Chesham Bois,
grandson of Thomas Cheyne, the Lollard.
The grandson and great-grandson of *this*
John Cheyne, Robert and John, were among
the staunchest Protestants in the district
in the days of Edward VI. and Elizabeth. It
was the latter who, in 1584, presented the illus-
trious Richard Hooker to the living of Drayton
Beauchamp, and there seems some reason to think
that he disinherited his own son for his adherence
to Romanism. (See the account of this interesting family by the late Rev. W. H. Kelke,
in the *Records of Buckinghamshire*, i. 293-301;
ii. 128-135).

The movement of 1414, whatever its real aims
may have been, must have taken a deep root in
the district to unite in its support the tradesmen
and yeomen from Wycombe and Amersham, the
squire's son from the manor-house of Drayton,
the priest from the secluded vale of Isenhamstead
Latimer, and the peasant who plucked, on the
lonely slopes of Wycombe Heath, the " grey goose
quills " which might be used next year by the
bowmen of Agincourt. Of course it is not certain
or likely that all of these Buckinghamshire sympathisers with the revolt were present at " Thicket
Field " by St. Giles's. The actions which led to
their arrest may have taken place in their own
neighbourhood.

In the same year (1414) Parliament, which

met at Leicester, " for the great favour that the
Lord Cobham had in London," passed a crushing
Act for the suppression of Lollardy, known as
" the Merciless Statute." Everyone convicted
of heresy was to forfeit his possessions; and an
oath was administered to all magistrates, from
the Lord Chancellor downwards, that he would
endeavour to extirpate " all manner of heresies,
errors, and Lollardies." It was not until 1625
that this oath was disused, the word " Lollardy "
being construed after the Reformation of any doctrines dangerous to public order. In the year
named, the great Sir Edward Coke, on being
appointed High Sheriff of Buckinghamshire,
declined to take the oath in this form, on the
ground (scarcely correct, by the way) that the
doctrines of the Lollards had been endorsed by
the Church of England; and this led to the dis-
continuance of the oath.

The later years of Henry V. were marked by
severe persecution. A prominent incident in
this was the cruel death of Sir John Oldcastle,
who, having been captured in Wales, was executed in St. Giles's Fields in February, 1418.
He was hanged in chains, and a fire was lighted
beneath him, so that he might be " hanged as
a traitor and burned as a heretic."

It is curious that not only did this intensely
Catholic King fail to suppress Lollardy, which
was still so strong at the close of his reign that
Archbishop Chichele said that nothing but an
armed force would put it down; but owing to

political exigencies, his reign was marked by the first great step in the interference of the State with monasticism. This was the suppression of the "alien priories." In Buckinghamshire, those of Newton Longville and Wing, with the hospital at Ludgershall, were suppressed in this reign. The property of Newton passed to New College, Oxford, and Wing was granted to a nunnery at St. Albans; but Ludgershall became Crown property. Tickford had already been suppressed by Edward III., though Henry IV. had restored it as a cell of a monastery near York.

The persecution continued after the accession of the child-king Henry VI. in 1422. In 1428, the year in which Wycliffe's bones were exhumed and burned to ashes at Lutterworth, a number of Lollards were compelled to abjure their belief in London. Among them as we read in Wilkins' *Concilia* (iii. 493) was one "Master Robert," parish priest of "Heggeley, in the diocese of Lincoln," who had formerly, it is said, been confessor to a certain "robber" named William Wawe, to whom other allusions occur at this period. Robert had long been imprisoned in the Tower, and on July 20th he was brought in chains before Chichele, sitting in Convocation, and questioned on the sacrament of the altar, pilgrimages, the worship of images, and the lawfulness of churchmen holding temporal lordships. His answers being unsatisfactory, he was committed to the custody of Bishop Fleming, and, though he abjured at Paul's Cross, was imprisoned

for life. There can be little doubt that " Heggeley " was Hedgerley in Bucks, a village about
seven miles south of Amersham.

About the same time Richard Monk, vicar of
Chesham, made his submission (Wilkins, iii.
302), and his recantation was read at Paul's Cross
in December of the same year. Foxe (iii. 538)
speaks of both Chesham and " Heggeley " as in
Lincolnshire, confusing the county with the
diocese.

In the spring of 1431, Humphrey, Duke of
Gloucester, the uncle of the young king, and
Protector of the kingdom, rode with men-at-arms
to Abingdon, to suppress an alleged Lollard
revolt. He seized the Bailiff of the town, William
Mandeville, who was accused of having threatened a general massacre of priests, and who was
hanged, drawn, and quartered, his head being
set on London Bridge. Another leader, Jack
Sharpe, arrested at Oxford, shared his fate. This
movement occurred near enough to the Buckinghamshire border to render it possible that
inhabitants of the county might take part; but
we have no proof that such was the case.

Lollardy was now burdened with the odium
of a supposed connection with four successive
revolts. How far this odium was deserved, is
very doubtful. The earliest of the four, the great
peasant rising under Richard II., was mainly due
as we have seen, to social and economic causes,
and it is significant that John of Gaunt, who up
till then had been Wycliffe's patron, was the

object of the fiercest hatred of the commons. Salisbury's rebellion against Henry IV. in 1400 was purely political, and was prompted by generous loyalty to a fallen king. We have already seen what uncertainty surrounds the real aims of the St. Giles's Fields rising in 1414. And it is impossible to say to what extent the obscure movement headed by Mandeville and Sharpe was really of Lollard origin, or whether, if it were so, there was any foundation for the violent purposes ascribed to it. There may be traced all through this period two distinct lines of influence often confused by opponents, and sometimes both affecting the same persons in varying degrees. The one was theological, and commenced with Wycliffe; the other socialistic, with a religious tinge, and commencing with men like Langland and Ball. Some of the Lollards seem to have held the doctrine of non-resistance; and if others erred in taking the carnal sword, they terribly atoned for their error. Anyhow, it is remarkable that no accusation of treason or disloyalty is brought against them after 1431. As with the Puritans after the Restoration, another work lay before them, more pacific, more obscure, but not less important.

Archbishop Trench, in his *Lectures on Mediæval Church History* (pp. 322, 323) speaks of 1431 as the date at which the persecution of the Lollards suddenly ceased. This is correct to a certain extent, though later researches have shown that occasional charges of heresy were made all through the century. Trench is inclined to ascribe the lull in the persecution to sheer weariness on the part of the persecutors. He admits that the " aggressive force " of Lollardy was spent; that the loss of Oxford, and the death or recantation of one after another of its leaders, had destroyed its academic and political influence, and that it was no longer " a power claiming recognition in Church and State, and in fact demanding that both should be fashioned and moulded according to its notions."

He goes on however to say :—

" But of its continued existence, not seeking any more to transform England at once, but to reach its ends by slower means, by the winning of one convert after another, abundant evidence remains. . . . . Large and open gatherings for the preaching of the Word were not indeed any more attempted.   The itinerant preacher had given place to the itinerant reader, who was never more active than at the close of the fifteenth and beginning of the sixteenth century.   There were little assemblies or conventicles everywhere ; and it might put to a wholesome shame our careless, unthankful use of Holy Scripture, to read how precious the Word in those days was ; how men came together by night, at peril of their lives, in lonely houses, in barns. in stables, to hear some tract which should expound that Word . . . . or oftener still, to listen to Scripture itself, a Gospel, or the Apocalypse, dear ever to those that suffer tribulation, or a Pauline Epistle, or, which

noticeably enough was a still more favourite
reading, the Epistle of St. James. And so the
Lollards lived on ; and when the Reformation came
at last, these humble men did much, as we may
well believe, to contribute to it that element of
sincerity, truth, and uprightness, without which
it never could have succeeded ; while yet, as must
be sorrowfully owned, this element was miserably
lacking in many who, playing foremost parts in
the carrying of a Reformation through, yet sought
in it not the things of God, but their own."

This estimate is far nearer the truth than that
of Froude, (i. 502), who speaks of the Lollard
movement as a mere " prologue " or "rehearsal "
of the drama of the Reformation, and asserts that
in the sixteenth century there remained no trace
of Lollardy save " a black memory of contempt
and hatred."

It must be borne in mind that there are few
periods of English history of which we have
scantier records than of the period from 1430 to
1480. The policy of the Inquisition had borne
its natural fruit in the suppression of all intellectual life. " Never before," says Mr. J. R.
Green, " had English literature fallen so low. A
few tedious moralists alone preserved the name
of poetry. History died down into the merest
fragments and annals. Even the religious enthusiasm of the people seemed to have spent itself,
or to have been crushed out by the bishops' courts.
The one belief of the time was in sorcery and
magic." A most fearful picture of the state of

the Church is drawn by Gascoigne, Chancellor
of Oxford, in a MS. referred to by Professor
Thorold Rogers in his *Six Centuries of Work and
Wages* (ch. xiii.). He says that many of the
monasteries deserved to be suppressed as dens
of gluttony, drunkenness, and vice; that the
Bishops of Salisbury, Norwich, and Carlisle, who
held high offices of state, were greedy, negligent,
and scandalous; and he casts serious imputations
on the moral character of the Archbishop of
Canterbury (John Stafford) himself.   He also
denounces with Luther-like vehemence the action
of Pope Eugenius IV., who in 1440, sent to
England an agent, named Pietro di Monte, for
the sale of indulgences. Yet it must not be forgotten that this dark period saw a seed sown in
Buckinghamshire soil, by the foundation of Eton
in 1440, which was destined to bear rich fruit in
after ages.

In 1439 a priest named Richard Wyche was
burned for heresy on Tower Hill.   Stow says
he was vicar of " Hermetsworth," by which he
no doubt means Harmondsworth, a parish in
Middlesex, bordering on the Bucks parish of Iver,
and within a few miles of Amersham and Chesham.   It would be interesting to connect Wyche
with the Lollard district, but there is reason to
think that Stow has confounded him with another
Richard Wyche, who was vicar of Harmondsworth a few years later, and that the martyr was
vicar of Deptford.   Wyche was over eighty years
of age.   He was very probably a pupil of Wycliffe,

and had almost certainly corresponded with John Huss. Immense interest was awakened after his death by the fact that a fragrant perfume arising from his ashes was distinctly perceptible. Pilgrims flocked to the scene of his martyrdom, and a rude stone monument was erected on the spot, placed there by unknown hands at night. But on inquiry it appeared that the vicar of the adjoining parish of Allhallows Barking had mixed spices with the ashes, in order to sell them to the people. A proclamation was issued forbidding resort to the place, and the affair was soon forgotten.

CHAPTER VII

UNDER THE WHITE ROSE OF YORK

ONE reason for the cessation of persecution referred to in the last chapter was probably the growing weakness of the House of Lancaster. The losses in France, the rebellion of Cade in 1450 (when there is no mention of religious grievances), and above all the outbreak of the Wars of the Roses in 1455, might all tend to make its supporters feel it impolitic to add to the number of its enemies. As Fuller beautifully says of the Lollards, "The very storm was their shelter." The murder by the populace of the Bishops of Salisbury and Chichester in 1450 would also tend to alarm and restrain the prelates, as they saw how thoroughly unpopular their order had become.

In the struggle over the succession we may be pretty sure that the sympathies of the Lollards would be with the House of York. They had assuredly no cause to love the Lancastrian kings; and it is noteworthy that the strength of the Yorkists lay in the districts where the Lollards were most numerous.

Yet as soon as Edward IV. was firmly estab-

lished on the throne, we find signs of a renewal
of persecution, and this affects the very parishes
in Buckinghamshire where Lollardy had been
so strong in 1414 and 1428.   In 1457, Edmund
Brudenell, lord of the manor of Amersham, had
bequeathed certain English Bibles (probably of
Wycliffe's version) to the University of Oxford
(See *Records of Bucks*, i. 297).   Now, in or about
1462, as appears by the Lincoln Register of Bishop Chedworth (fol. 62, *a.t.*), proceeedings for
heresy were taken against persons who had
probably been tenants of Brudenell's—John
Baron, Geoffrey Symeon, John Crane, and Robert
Body, of Agmondesham (Amersham).   Their
confessions are very interesting.

Baron had been acquainted with one Hugh
Leche, who held " a damnable opinion against
pilgrimages and the worshipping of saints," and
who taught that it was sufficient for salvation to
keep the ten commandments, and that the sacrament of the altar was mere bread.   He had also
listened many times to William Belgrave, and to
John White of Chesham, who " taught and held
many heresies against the seven sacraments of
Holy Church."   Baron owned to the possession
of three books in English.   The first contained
" The Life of our Lady," " The Mirror of
Sinners," and " The Mirror of Matrimony,"
with sermons on Adam and Eve and other subjects.   The second was " a book of Tales of
Canterbury " (no doubt Chaucer's), and the third
was " a play of St. Dionise."   The very posses-

sion of an English book seems to have been
regarded as suspicious. Questioned as to his own
views, Baron admitted that he had listened with
pleasure to Leche's teaching, and had given
"faith, credence, and belief" to his views as
to pilgrimages and image-worship, holding that
to do good to the poor was better "than to seek
or worship any saint or image on earth." But
he denied having held any heretical doctrine as
to the sacraments. He had kept his views to
himself, except when he had talked them over
with a friend named Spicer. Baron now sued
for mercy, and submitted to the correction of the
Church, as did also Symeon, Crane, and Body.

Geoffrey Symeon had learned his views from one
James Wylly, who had given him "an English
book of the Holy Gospels," and who had afterwards been burned as a heretic in London. He
had also known John White of Chesham, who
was "diffamed of heresy"; and when William
Sparman, the Bishop's officer, had come to Amersham to seek for heretics, he and Body had given
White warning. His statement of his views was
similar to Baron's, with one curious addition. "I
have dogmatised," he said, "that bishops should
go on foot with twelve priests, clothed as the
sheep beareth all in white, teaching the people
the true Christian faith; but they teach the people
that is false and untrue, against God's law."
There may be here a dim reminiscence of the
Poor Priests, whose gowns of "russet" were
made of undyed *black* wool.

John Crane had been conversant with persons
"noised and suspect of heresy," and had even
found an heretical adviser in a parish priest, the
parson of Chesham Bois, by whose "counsel and
motion" he had left off giving his alms.

Robert Body (whose surname is still a common
one in the district) had been "conversant with
heretics, hearing their dogmatizations, hiding and
keeping their counsels, and giving them warning
when William Sparman and other officers of the
Bishop's came into the country to seek them."

The Bishop of Lincoln had at this time a
stately country seat at Wooburn, in Buckinghamshire (to be carefully distinguished from the
better known Woburn in Beds). Here on August
21st, 1462, John Polley, of Henley-on-Thames,
abjured before Bishop Chedworth, and promised
to give information of any heretical persons or
books he might know of for the future, after
which he received the Bishop's absolution. Polley
had disbelieved in purgatory and transubstantiation, had objected to images in churches, and
had held that the offerings made to them had
better be given to the poor.   "Also that the
sacrament of Baptime doon with the observaunces
of the Churche and in the fonte is not necessary ;
but to crysten a child rather in a Ryver or a
ponde."

On October 11th another Henley heretic was
cited before the Bishop in High Wycombe Church,
which had lately been greatly adorned and beauti-
fied. "All the piers and arches, the roofs in the

nave, the aisles, and the clerestory windows,"
show early fifteenth-century work. It was about
four years later that the wealthy burgess William
Redehode adorned the church with elaborately
carved oak screens. An inventory taken in 1475,
and preserved in Parker's *History and Antiquities
of Wycombe* (p. 106) gives a vivid idea of the
ritual of those days. It will be read with a sigh
of regret by those ecclesiastical sentimentalists
who mourn over the vanished glories of the past
(while they sometimes seem to have no regrets
to spare for the defacement of the living temples
of the Holy Ghost by the flame, the branding-
iron, and the quartering-knife).   We read of
vestments of costly brocade, one suit of red,
embroidered with golden-damask foliage, with
birds and lions ; another of blue, wrought with
green branches and golden birds ; another with
golden birds on a ground of white. Other suits
were of stuff, with green and gold foliage ;
of red velvet, with golden crowns ; of
green velvet ; of red silk, with white
embroidery ; of cloth of gold ; of blue silk,
with golden rays ; and one of black for requiem
masses. There were seven chasubles, one embroidered with golden apes, sporting amid violet
branches ; another with golden birds on a red
ground.   There were white and black copes, with
embroidery of blue and gold, presented by
William Redehode ; long "houselling" towels
for the administration of the sacrament ; cushions
of silk and brocade ; palls, and veils, and lectern-

cloths. Of the altar-cloths, one had golden squirrels and green foliage on a black ground. Another was similiar, but with hinds instead of squirrels. Others were of imitation cloth of gold, or of blue worsted with golden flowers and silver spangles. There were silken banners, on one of which the Trinity was depicted on a blue ground ; silken pennons and pendants ; rich canopies, one of purple silk with gilded ornaments, another of lawn, with a fringe of red and gold ; curtains of blue sarsenet and purple silk ; and a cloth of gold to cover the " sepulchre." Six silver chalices, all but one gilt, were provided for the service of the altar, with patens to correspond. Two candlesticks of latten (fine brass) stood on the high altar, two very large ones in the choir, and two more in St. Nicholas' chancel. There were various other ornaments of silver, as candlesticks, basons, " shippes " and " crewettes," besides censers with silver chains. The pax was of silver gilt, set with jewels ; and there were costly reliquaries, and several crosses, one of which was of copper gilt, set with precious stones. Lastly, a number of service-books are mentioned, some of them no doubt in costly bindings.

Into the midst of these imposing splendours was brought, on the date above mentioned, William Aylward of Henley, master blacksmith. The Wars of the Roses were not ended. The battle of Hexham had been fought a few months before. But the pilgrims still went on their way to the shrine of St. Thomas at Canterbury. Some little time before, as some of them were passing Aylward's forge on their way through Henley town, the smith, at work with his men, Robert Noris and William Assheley, bluntly remarked, "They go offering their souls to the devil." He also talked to his men about the Gospel of Nicodemus, an apocryphal book which Wycliffe had translated. From hearing it read (for he does not seem to have been able to read or write) he had come to the conclusion that "the sacrament of baptism at the font was only a token and a sign," and "that no man ought to be baptised till he came to old age." Other charges were based on random utterances of his at different times, coarse and blasphemous enough, but showing the natural revolt of a vigorous but untaught mind against the teachings of Rome. The blood of Hales, he said, was that of a dog or a duck, and the miracle of its liquefaction was visible, not as the monks taught to the pure in heart, but to those who paid a sufficient offering. Of the Mass, he had spoken in terms which will hardly bear transcription, and had said, " I can make as good a sacrament myself between two irons ; for a priest neither can nor may make God that made him." Confession, he said, was only maintained by the priests for purposes of immorality. His audacious tongue had spared neither the Pope nor the King. Of the former he had said that "he would lie deeper in hell than Lucifer ;" and he declared that the King also would go to hell " because of his great support-ation of the Church." But this charge was passed over in silence by the Bishop, with the consent of the Lord Chancellor, the Bishop of Exeter. Probably this was to prevent the intervention of a secular court; but whatever the motive, it was an act of mercy on which Aylward might well congratulate himself, since it probably saved him from being hung, drawn, and quartered as a traitor.

Aylward had learned his views, he said, from one named "Patryk." He had been in trouble some years before for sorcery—in other words for professing to cure children of the whooping-cough by dipping his second finger into water into which a red-hot steelyard had been plunged, and bidding the parents say five Paternosters and five Ave Marias. But the charges against him now were much more serious. They were read over to him, and as he pleaded "Guilty" to each in turn, the word *fatetur* (he confesses) was entered against it. Aylward had evidently nothing of the martyr spirit, and readily abjured his reckless utterances, which seem to have been prompted more by a love of shocking his neighbours than by any higher motives. Having thus abjured, he received absolution, but would no doubt have to do penance. It is a pitiful picture—priestly intolerance on the one hand, and on the other blind, ignorant fanaticism of that extreme type which is generally fostered by persecution. But a change was at hand. More than one of those who were charged with heresy in the days of

Henry VII. and VIII. fixed the latter part of the reign of Edward IV. as the period of their conversion to Lollard views. And we shall soon see indications that Lollard teachers were probably at work in the Chiltern country at this time, though all record of their labours has perished.

CHAPTER VIII

THE REVIVAL OF LOLLARDY

WHEN Henry VII. took the crown of the usurper Richard from the hawthorn-bush of Bosworth Field in 1485, and when he afterwards ended the strife of the Roses by marrying the Princess Elizabeth, he seems to have resolved not only to unite the two Houses of York and Lancaster, but to combine their characteristic policies—the personal rule of Edward IV. with the rigid churchmanship of the Lancastrian Kings.

At the very beginning of his reign, cases of " heresy " are recorded at London and Coventry. Lollard doctrines, too, had once more found their way into Oxford. In 1491, Bishop Russell of Lincoln, visiting that city, declared himself " harassed and fatigued " with the multitude of heretics he found there. He betook himself to his episcopal seat at Wooburn, mentioned in the last chapter; and there he made a copy of a work called the *Doctrinale*, by Thomas Netter of Walden, which he considered would be of service to his successors in dealing with heretics. The MS. (according to Dr. Churton's *Founders of Brasenose* p. 134) is preserved in the library

of University College; it bears an autograph
injunction for its perpetual preservation in the
registry of Lincoln, with a curse on any one
defacing this injunction, which is dated " Wooburn, on the Feast of the Epiphany, 1491 " (1492
of our present reckoning).

About eight miles from Wooburn, in another
lovely valley among the beech-crowned slopes of
the Chilterns, lies the little town of Amersham,
already more than once referred to.   In Foxe's
account of Thomas Man, burned in Smithfield
in 1518, he mentions (iv. 213) that Man, after
many wanderings, came to Newbury from Windsor Forest, and was there told of the existence
of a number of Lollards at Amersham.   Thither
he went accordingly, and found " a godly and
a great company," who had continued in their
belief for twenty-three years.   This would take
us back to 1495 at the latest.   Foxe did not know
that, as we have seen was the case, Lollard principles were strong in and around Amersham in
1414, in 1428, and again in 1462.   No wonder
that the town should have become a stronghold
of Lollard principles—" the rendezvous of God's
children in those days," as Fuller calls it.

Everything seems to point to a great revival
of Lollard doctrine about this time (1495).   The
date itself is suggestive.   Henry VII. had been
ten years on the throne.   The Papal Court had
sunk to its lowest depth of degradation in the
Borgia Pope, Alexander VI.   Savonarola was at
the zenith of his influence at Florence.   Luther

was a singing boy in the streets of Eisnach.
Three years before, two great events had stirred
the heart of Europe with hopes unknown to it
for ages. The constant stealthy advance of
Mohammedanism, which had blasted three-fourths
of Christendom, had at last met with a check
in the capture of Granada; and in the same year
the daring of Christopher Columbus had revealed
the New World of America. The discovery of
printing had marvellously aided the spread of
knowledge; and now the "New Learning,"
brought into Italy by Grecian refugees after the
taking of Constantinople by the Turks, had
reached the shores of England. Two years later
Colet commenced his New Testament lectures at
Oxford, and the long lethargy which had paralysed
the University since the time of Courtenay began
at last to be broken.

John Colet was of an old Buckinghamshire
family. Lipscombe (ii. 431) says that he was
born at Wendover; but most authorities give London as the place of his birth. He certainly owned
extensive landed property in Wendover and the
adjoining parishes, which he bequeathed to St.
Paul's School. Here again we find ourselves just
on the borders of the old Lollard district; and it
is impossible to say what influences may
have affected him from this fact. Erasmus
hints that Colet had made himself familiar
with Wycliffe's writings; and though he
calls the Lollards "men mad with strange folly,"
Colet was not the first or the last ecclesiastic who

was far nearer than he suspected in spiritual affinity to despised sectaries whose real standpoint he scarcely understood.

Colet's simplicity of life, his Scriptural teaching, and his manly protests against the evils of the day, would naturally commend him to the Lollards; and hence we can quite believe Foxe when he tells us (iv. 246) that "these 'known men' about Buckinghamshire had a great mind to resort to his sermons" after he was apponted Dean of St. Paul's (1505). His friend and fellow-reformer Grocyn, it may be noted in passing, at one time had been rector of a Buckinghamshire parish, Newton Longville.

"Heretics" were being brought to light with increasing frequency over various parts of the south of England. In 1494 the first English female martyr, Joan Boughton, was burned in Smithfield. A priest was burned at Canterbury in 1498, and another victim suffered at Norwich in 1500. In the diocese of Salisbury, numerous persons were compelled to do penance in various parts of Berkshire (1499). Their confessions, preserved in the Diocesan Register, are mostly of the ordinary Lollard type. Eight cases are recorded at Reading, six in and around Faringdon, five in Wantage and the neighbourhood, and one at Hungerford. We shall find presently that there was constant communication between these Berkshire Lollards and their brethren across the Thames in Bucks.

CHAPTER IX

THREE LOLLARD TEACHERS AND THEIR FATE

As we have now to a large extent to follow the guidance of John Foxe, it will be necessary to say a few words on the credibility of that author, who has been so depreciated in modern days that one is almost afraid to mention him—

Lest so despised a name should move a sneer.

It may be freely conceded that Foxe is in many respects an unreliable writer, ever ready to put the blackest construction on the actions of theological opponents, and to gloss over facts which tell against his own side; but he lived in an age which did not understand the meaning of critical fairness. It must also be admitted that his work absolutely swarms with blunders, especially as to dates; but it must be borne in mind that the greater part of it was written on the Continent, in the altogether inadequate space, for a work of such extent, in fourteen months; and while Foxe corrected some of his more glaring errors in subsequent editions, the traces of its original hurry of compilation still remain on the book.

No book has had stranger fortunes than the

Acts and Monuments. Christened as soon as it
appeared by a name (the " Book of Martyrs ")
which its author never gave it, and against which
he protested again and again as misrepresenting
its scope, it has had its rightful title entirely
supplanted by a nickname. Received at first with
extravagant admiration, ordered to be set up in
every parish church, and in the common halls of
archbishops, bishops, deans, and heads of col-
leges ; approved by the great Elizabethan prelates
(one of whom, Archbishop Grindal, furnished
Foxe with many of his details) ; quoted with
admiration by men like Camden, Strype, Fuller,
and Burnet ; it has come in our own day to be as
much undervalued as it was overvalued then. For
although the searching light of criticism has exposed Foxe's prejudices and inaccuracies, some of
the attacks upon him have been so grossly unfair,
and themselves so absolutely uncritical, as to make
one wonder whether, after all, the great offence
of the " lying Foxe," in the eyes of some modern
partisans, is not that he tells more truth than is
convenient for them. Froude's testimony is
worth quoting : " I trust Foxe where he pro-
duces documentary evidence, because I have in-
variably proved his documents accurate." And
a careful reader of the elaborate notes in Pratt
and Stoughton's edition will observe that such
departures from his original documents as do occur
are almost always those which might arise either
from hasty transcription or from ignorance of
technical terms.

Foxe's references to Buckinghamshire occur for the first time in his second edition (1570). He does not appear to have had any close personal acquaintance with the county. Some local writers have suggested that the John Fox who was Vicar of Stewkley in 1545, may have been the same as the martyrologist. This, however, seems impossible; for in that year Foxe left Oxford, under suspicion of heresy, and became a tutor at Charlecote Park, Warwickshire, whence, a year later, he removed to Coventry.

Foxe tells us (iv. 123) how, in the year 1506, the Amersham Lollards attracted the attention of Bishop William Smith (the successor of Russell in the see of Lincoln, and founder of Brasenose College, Oxford), who instituted proceedings against them. Amersham, or Agmondesham as it was then called, is now one of the quietest and sleepiest of towns, until recently seven miles from a railway station. But it was then of greater relative importance. Being twenty-six miles from London on an important road, it would be a favourite halting-place for wayfarers, and news from the metropolis would reach it quickly. Thus the Lollards there would soon get to know of the preaching of Colet. We read (Foxe, iv. 228) how " Thomas Grove, of London, butcher, William Glasbroke, of Harrow-on-the-Hill, Christopher Glasbroke, of London, and William Tilseworth, of London, goldsmith (apprentice sometime to John Barret) used to resort and confer together of matters of religion in the house of Thomas Man,

of Amersham," about this time. These visitors
from London would be glad of a secluded spot in
which to confer with their co-religionists; and
they would be likely to follow the example of
Thomas Geffrey, of Uxbridge, who " caused John
Butler divers Sundays to go to London to hear
Dr. Colet " (iv. 230).

These Lollards were some of them men of
substance. Of Thomas Grove, we read (iv. 227)
that he was able to give £20, a large sum for
those days, to Dr. Wilcocks, Vicar-General of
the diocese of London, in order to be excused
from an open penance. He and his wife Joan
seem afterwards to have lived at Amersham (iv.
233); and the surname is still familiar in the district. As to William Tilseworth, the goldsmith,
it is curious to notice, all through the history of
the Lollards, how many goldsmiths belonged to
the body; and the goldsmith in those days was
an important personage, for he frequently acted
as a banker. His master, John Barret, knew the
Epistle of James by heart, and repeated it on one
occasion before his wife Joan, and her maid Jude,
and a visitor, John Scrivener, to whom Mistress
Barret also lent the Gospels of Matthew and
Mark, which he surrendered to Bishop Smith
(iv. 228).

The Amersham Lollards had at this time three
" principal readers or instructors "—William
Tylsworth, or Tilseworth (Tylesley in the edition
of 1570), Robert Cosin, and Thomas Chase.

William Tylsworth was very possibly the

father of the young man who had been apprenticed
to the pious goldsmith Barret. He had called the
images of the saints " stocks and stones and dead
things" (iv. 221). He was sentenced to be burned,
and the sentence was carried out in a field called
Stanley's Close, still pointed out on a slope north
of the town. About sixty Lollards, the names of
over twenty of whom are given by Foxe (iv. 123)
were " put to bear faggots for their penance " at
his burning. We can picture them climbing the
hill in slow and sad procession, while numbers
of the townspeople and even of their children
followed with faggots and sticks in order to merit
the forty days' indulgence which had been promised to all who should assist at the burning of
the heretic (iv. 581). By a refinement of cruelty
when the faggots had been piled around the stake,
his only daughter, Joan Clark, " a faithful
woman," was compelled to set fire to them with
her own hands, while her husband John Clark
was one of the faggot-bearers. Thus Tylsworth met his end with every aggravation of
physical and mental agony, and of apparent utter
failure in his work ; but in his case, as in that of
countless others, the saying was to be verified :
" The blood of the martyrs is the seed of the
Church."

A curious variation from Foxe's account occurs
in one of the numerous " Books of Martyrs "
based on his work, which was compiled early in
the nineteenth century by a Dr. Henry Moore.
We there read as follows :—" In 1506, William

Tilfery, a pious man, was burnt alive at Amersham, in a close called Stony-prat." This evidently refers to the case of Tylsworth, and it is curious that the name of Stony Prat is still given to a field lying to the north of Amersham. The local traditions, however, gather neither around this nor around Stanleys, but around a field called Ruckles, or Martyr Field, which lies between the two, not far from the railway station. It is possible that the present enclosures did not then exist, so that Ruckles would form part of Stanleys. Beyond Ruckles to the westward lies the " Tenter Field " before alluded to, and beyond this again, on the other side of the Chesham road, is Stony Prat. As the traveller approaches Amersham from the south, and looks across the valley in which the quaint old town nestles, little changed in extent and appearance, comparatively speaking, by the four centuries which have elapsed, he sees a hilly field (Ruckles) under the beech-woods on the opposite slope, and in it a slight depression where, it used to be said, the corn would never grow, but always faded away. Some years ago as I learned from the late Mr. E. West, so well and honourably known in the town, the Rev. Joseph Burton, a retired West Indian missionary, who was then pastor of the Lower Baptist Chapel at Amersham, employed a labouring man named Belch to dig up the soil, and found that an old chalk-pit had been filled up with large flints, thus accounting for the barrenness of the site. Belch died shortly after, and not a few looked on his death as a visitation of God ! A few years later, a local solicitor, the late Mr. Thomas Marshall, repeated the experiment, and confirmed the conclusion arrived at by the Baptist minister. This time the flints were partly removed, and since then the ground has been less barren, but it still shows a difference from the surrounding soil in a dry season. The spot was probably chosen for the place of execution as a piece of waste ground, visible from all parts of the town ; and its conspicuous barrenness has preserved the memory of the site to successive generations.

Several members of the Tylsworth family are mentioned as suspected of heresy a few years later. I have not traced the name in the district, though " Tyldesley " occurs on a monument in Burnham Church. The name of Clark, on the other hand, is common in the county, and was borne by an old Bucks family of Quakers.

In the same week as Tylsworth suffered, his fellow-worker, Robert Cosin, was burned at Buckingham. He was a miller, living at Missenden, and was familiarly known as " Father Robert." Cosin appears to have been condemned for dissuading his neighbours from pilgrimages and the worship of saints. At his burning more than twenty persons were compelled to bear faggots as a penance. Dr. Moore, in the work just now alluded to, states, on what authority does not appear, that Cosin, or Roberts as he calls him, " embraced the faggots, and rejoiced that God had accounted him worthy to die for the truth of the Gospel."

The third Lollard leader in the district at this time was Thomas Chase. Here again we come upon a name familiar in the district. The Chases, or one branch of them, lived for generations at the quaint old manor-house of Hundridge, near Chesham, and were connected with the Lower Baptist Chapel in that town. This branch have now removed to the States, and their American home is, I am told, built on the plan, and bears the name of Hundridge, while some of them visit the Buckinghamshire homestead from time to time.

Thomas Chase appears to have been of a somewhat more timid disposition than Tylsworth and Cosin. He had exhorted one of the persons to whom he taught passages of Scripture, " to keep the things he spake of as secret in his stomach as a man would keep a thief in prison " (iv. 225). Like Barret the goldsmith, he could recite the Epistle of James, and also part at least of the Gospel of Luke (iv. 224). He seems to have yielded before the first onslaught of persecution, and bore a faggot at Tylsworth's martyrdom. But a little later he was taken from Amersham to Wooburn, and examined before Bishop Smith. He now atoned for his previous weakness by a courageous confession, and was imprisoned in the " Little Ease " adjoining the Bishop's palace at Wooburn, a prison in which it was impossible for him to stand upright, or to lie down with comfort; although it is to be hoped that the ghastly picture of the Wooburn dungeon drawn by Miss Holt in her *Robin Tremayne* does not quite correspond with the actual fact. "Little Ease" was the name of a well-known cell in the Tower of London, and was applied to others in various parts of the country. Foxe states that Chase was loaded with "chains, gyves, manacles, and irons," beaten, half starved, and daily harassed with threats and upbraidings by the Bishop's chaplains. At last, finding that he would not recant, his persecutors tortured him more severely than ever, and finally strangled him. The woman who attended to the prisoner was within earshot, and heard his groans, and his dying cry, "Lord Jesus, receive my spirit!" It does not appear that his death had been intended; and his tormentors were "at their wits' end" for means to conceal their cruelty. They gave out that Chase had hanged himself in prison—a physical impossibility, considering the height of the cell, and the chains with which he was loaded. However, he was buried as a suicide on the road from Wooburn to Little Marlow, in the wood called Norland (now Northern) Wood.

Such is Foxe's account, stripped of his usual violent epithets of "stinging vipers," "bloody butchers," etc., applied to Chase's persecutors. A local writer, a few years ago, expressed his opinion that Chase really hanged himself, and that the "martyr-on-the-brain-affected Foxe" supplied "the agony accompaniment" out of his fertile imagination. This may be a matter of opinion, but when the writer in question goes on to say (quoting Lysons' *Buckinghamshire*, but not mentioning his authority) that the Bishop is " ably defended by Dr. Churton, of Brasenose, and by Fuller in his *Church History*," he gives a striking example of the pitfalls in the way of a superficial inquiry, for one of the authorities referred to accepts Foxe's account implicitly ; and the other does so hesitatingly, but seeks to exonerate the Bishop, whom Foxe never accused of being concerned in Chase's death. The matter is worth looking at more closely, as an example of the facile way in which Foxe is sometimes discredited on no evidence at all.

Fuller (*Church History*, book v., p. 164), after speaking favourably of Smith's apparent clemency in substituting branding for burning in certain cases, goes on to say :—

" They who desire further information of the number and names of such as suffered about this time may repair to the *Acts and Monuments* of Mr. Foxe ; only Thomas Chase, of Amersham, must not be here omitted, being barbarously butchered by bloudy hands in the Prison of Wooburne ; who, to cover their cruelty, gave it out that he had hanged himself, and in colour thereof, caused his body to be buried by the highway's side, where a stake, knock't into the grave, is the monument generally erected for *Felons de se*. ' Fear not those ' (saith our Saviour) ' who kill the body, and afterward have no more that they can do.' But these men's malice endeavoured to do more, having killed his body, to murder his memory with slanderous reports, although all in vain; for the prison itself did plead for the innocence of the prisoner herein, being a place so low and little that he could not stand upright. Besides, the woman that saw his dead body (a most competent witness in this case) declared that he was so loaden with manicles and irons that he could not well move hand or foot. But we leave the full discussing and final deciding to Him who makes inquisition for bloud, at that day when such things as have been done in secret shall be made manifest."

Turning now to Dr. Churton's *Founders of Brasenose* (pp. 137—140), we find him simply pointing out that Foxe cites no documents as to the deaths of Chase and Tylsworth, that the accounts he received were probably coloured and exaggerated with the lapse of time, and that Foxe himself elsewhere admits the comparative leniency of Smith, as to whom Churton avows his belief that " although the sentence might be his " (probably referring to Tylsworth's case) " the studied barbarity which disgraced the execution was the result of baser minds, without his suggestion or concurrence."

A small recess or cell in the cellarage of Wooburn House (which occupies nearly the site of the Bishop's palace) is pointed out as the " Lollards' Chamber " or " Little Ease." But it does not at all correspond with Foxe's description; and I believe that a more likely spot used

to be shown in some outbuildings now pulled
down. An aged lady once told me of a story she
had heard from her mother when living at Wooburn as a child, about certain martyrs who were
buried in the ground up to their necks in Northern
Woods, and left to starve—perhaps a distorted
version of the story of Chase.

CHAPTER X

THE GREAT ABJURATION

WE have seen that about eighty persons abjured
and did penance at the burning of Tylsworth and
Cosin. This wholesale abjuration of the Lollards
seems to have been that long remembered in the
district as *Magna Abjuratio*, " the Great Abjuration," and took place in 1507 (iv. 214). Another
followed in 1511, and to this the name is applied
in a marginal note, only found in some editions
of Foxe ; but most of the passages seem evidently
to refer to the earlier date.

It must be confessed that it is somewhat dis-
appointing, all through the history of the Lollards,
to notice the large proportion of abjurations.
Many of those who suffered during the fifteenth
and sixteenth centuries were condemned for
" relapse," *i.e.*, continuing in their views after
having once formally abjured. But it is probable
that some of the more stedfast souls were condemned to imprisonment, the protracted sufferings
of which may have been harder to bear than a
fiery martyrdom. Nor is it easy for us to estimate
the courage required to stand against the force

of an almost unchallenged authority. To quote
Coleridge's lines on the recantation of Berenga-
rius :—

> Ye who, secure 'mid trophies not your own,
> Judge him who won them when he stood
>   alone,
> And proudly talk of *recreant* Berengare,
> O first the age, and then the man compare !
> That age how dark ! congenial minds how
>   rare !
> No host of friends with kindred zeal did burn !
> No throbbing hearts awaited his return !
> Prostrate alike when prince and peasant fell,
> He only, disenchanted from the spell,
> Like the weak worm that gems the starless
>   night,
> Moved in the scanty circlet of his light ;
> And was it strange if he withdrew the ray
> That did but guide the night-birds to their
>   prey ?

The Marian martyrs were sustained by the con-
sciousness that a widespread and influential
public opinion, which often manifested itself in
active sympathy, was on their side. The "known
men " of Amersham had no such support, and
must often have doubted whether, after all, they,
a few unlettered people, could be right in holding
a belief which seemed contrary to that of all the
wise and learned of the land.
   The writer of an article in the *Spectator* of

Dec. 17th, 1892, says of similar recantations, recorded in diocesan registers :—

" We cannot help wondering in what spirit most of these recantations were made. Sometimes the profession of future orthodoxy may have been genuine. A man may have been startled to find that opinions he had held were heretical, and when the bishop bade him recant

> ' Lest thou fleet
> From my first to God's second death,'

he may have dreaded the spiritual penalty no less than the temporal one. Yet it is difficult to believe in the good faith of men who for years had belonged to a secret sect, who had scoffed at Church ordinances and avoided confession, but who declare in the most innocent way that now they understand their opinions to be false, and accordingly forsake them. . . . . . . The spirit of martyrs was not to be expected from these men, who had been trained for years to shelter themselves under an outward conformity . . . . For the time all aggressiveness and open proselytism had died out among the reformers, and it needed a new impulse to make them brave enough to bear public witness to the truth that they prized for themselves."

The Buckinghamshire Lollards did not escape with merely bearing faggots at the martyrdoms of Tylsworth and Cosin. Some of them had to do public penance in the market-places of Aylesbury and other towns. They were compelled to wear badges of green cloth on their sleeves, as a permanent mark of disgrace. Some were branded on the cheek. Fuller's words may be quoted here (*Church History*, book v., pp. 163, 164) :—

" At the same time sixty professors, and above, did bear fagots for their penance, and were enjoyned to wear on their right sleeve, for some years after, a square piece of cloth, as a disgrace to themselves, and a difference from others. But what is most remarkable, a new punishment was now found out—of branding them on the cheek. The manner thus : their necks were tied fast to a post with towels, and their hands holden that they might not stir; and so the hot iron was put to their cheeks. It is not certain whether branded with L, for Lollard, or H, for Heretick, or whether it was only a formless print of iron (yet nevertheless painful). This is sure, that they bare in their bodies the marks of the Lord Jesus. And no doubt they had so well learned our Saviour's precept, that rather than they would have revenged themselves by unlawful means, to them that smit them on the one cheek they would have turned the other also. Surely Ecclesiastical Constitutions did not reach thus far as to impose any corporal torture ; and whether there be any Statute of the Land that enjoyns (not to say permits) such punishments, let the learned in the Laws decide. This I am sure, if this was the first time they fell into this (supposed) Heresie, by the law they were onely to abjure their errours; and if it were the second time, upon relaps into the same again, their whole bodies were to be burnt. Except any will say, that such as by these bloudy Laws deserved death were branded onely by the favour of William Smith, Bishop of Lincoln; and one may have charity to encline him to this belief, when considering the same William (Founder of Brasenose Colledg in Oxford) was generally a lover of learning and goodness, and not cruelly disposed of himself."

This is the passage already referred to in the previous chapter. Fuller goes on :—

"However, some of God's children, though burnt, did not dread the fire. And Father Rever, *alias* Reive, though branded at the time, did afterwards suffer at a stake; so that the brand at the first did but take livery and seisin in his cheek, in token that his whole body should afterwards be in the free and full possession of the fire."

Another portion of the penance enjoined was a pilgrimage once or twice a year to certain shrines. Some of these were in Buckinghamshire —the shrine of Sir John Shorne at North Marston, that of St. Rumbold at Buckingham, of Our Lady at Missenden, or the famous crucifix known as the Holy Rood of Wendover. Other penitents had to take longer journeys, to trudge mile after mile into the low-lying lands beyond the Ouse, till they saw the towers of Lincoln rise before them on the hill; or to " Our Lady of Walsingham," the fashionable place of pilgrimage at this date, where Queen Catherine returned thanks a few years later for the victory of Flodden Field. The little Norfolk town, the abode of " the Virgin by the Sea " (*Virgo Parathalassia*), was so honoured that the country people, as they looked up at the starry sky, pointed at the Galaxy as " the Walsingham Way," intended to guide pilgrims to

> " The holy land
> Of blessed Walsingham."

It derived its chief title to reverence from a vial containing a white substance, which was shown as the Virgin's milk !

These pilgrimages were in some cases enjoined for seven successive years, and it would seem that on arriving at the shrines the penitents had again publicly to bear faggots on their shoulders. Robert Bartlet, a wealthy farmer, was kept seven years a prisoner in the College of the Precious Blood at Ashridge. " Father Rogers " (the surname occurs long after as that of a prominent Nonconformist family at Amersham) was not only branded on the right cheek, but confined for fourteen weeks in the Bishop's prison, probably at Wooburn, " where he was so cruelly handled with cold, hunger, and irons, that after his coming out of the said prison, he was so lame in his back that he could never go upright as long as he lived."

Foxe gives as his vouchers for this persecution of 1506-7 an aged man and woman—William

Littlepage and Agnes Wetherly, who were still
living when he wrote in 1570. Littlepage, whose
singular name occurs more than once in the list
of the Mayors of Wycombe, and in other local
records from 1475 to 1618, had borne a faggot,
while still a youth, at the martyrdom of Tylsworth, and had been branded on the cheek. He
had been apprenticed to John Scrivener, who did
penance at the same time (iv. 123, 225). Agnes
Wetherly must have been already in middle life
at the time of these events, if, as Foxe says, she
was nearly a hundred when he wrote. We can
imagine with what reverent interest these vene-
rable links with the past would be regarded in
the "spacious times of great Elizabeth;" but
their statements must evidently be received with
some reserve; and in fact, the whole of this part
of Foxe's narrative is more confused and contra-
dictory than we shall find it later on. For
example, he says (iv. 124), "After that" (i.e.,
the burning of Tylsworth and Cosin in 1506),
"by the space of two or three years, were burned
at Amersham, Thomas Barnard, a husbandman,
and James Morden, a labourer; they two were
burned both at one fire." This would make the
date 1508 or 1509. Yet on page 245 the names
of Thomas Bernard and James Morden are given
among those who suffered for relapse in 1521.
As both gave evidence in the Bishop's court in
the latter year, the earlier date cannot possibly
be the correct one. But to make the perplexity
greater still, on turning to vol. v., p. 454, we find

the same two men described as suffering in the
persecution following the issue of the Six Articles
(1539-1542). In the Kalendar prefixed to vol.
i., too, 1542 is the date given for their death.
But Foxe goes on to say that they were burned,
" the one for teaching the Lord's Prayer in English, and the other for keeping the Epistle of
St. James translated into English." Now, as
Maitland points out in his able but virulent criti-
cisms on Foxe in his *Essays on the Reformation*,
neither of these acts was illegal at the time of
the Six Articles. We may pretty safely conclude,
not, as Maitland seems to think, that the whole
story was a myth, but that Bernard and Morden
suffered in 1521, when we shall see their story
more clearly outlined. Burnet, by the way, says
that they suffered at Lincoln; but this is probably
a hasty assumption from Foxe's language in
vol. v.

The excitement which the persecution had
created in the little town of Amersham gradually
cooled down, but the "heresy" was far from
being stamped out. Thomas Holmes was heard
to mutter, "The greatest cobs are yet behind."
Roger Squire, seeing one of the informers who
had "detected" the accused, bitterly exclaimed,
"This is one of them that make all this business
in our town with the Bishop; I pray God tear
all the bones of him." As long after in Puritan
days, these informers became marked men.
People refused to have dealings with them; and
the gossips pointed out how one and another of

them was "brought now to beggary." Others said that those who had recanted "were good men and perfect Christians, and simple folk who could not answer for themselves, and therefore were oppressed by power of the Bishop."

Further abjurations would seem to have taken place in 1508 (iv. 221), and again in 1511 (iv. 226, margin). Thurstan Littlepage and Alexander Mastall are mentioned as leaders of the Amersham Lollards about this period; but Foxe is never very strong on dates. Bishop Smith showed himself increasingly averse to persecution, and mitigated the penance of some of the abjurers. Instead of the toilsome journey of a hundred miles to Lincoln, they were permitted to go to " Our Lady of Missenden," five miles only from Amersham. This indulgence, however, was refused to others. One man was allowed to "buy out his penance, and carry his badge in his purse."

In 1514 Bishop Smith passed away. The news was received by the Lollards with much anxiety, for it was doubtful if his successor would be as lenient. Richard White, of Beaconsfield, was heard to say, " My Lord that is dead was a good man, and divers known men were called before him, and he sent them home again, bidding them that they should live among their neighbours as good Christian men should do. And now there is a new Bishop, who is called a blessed man ; and if he be as he is named, he will not trouble the servants of God, but will let them be in quiet."

This " blessed man " was possibly no other
than Thomas Wolsey, afterwards Cardinal, who
held the see of Lincoln as well as that of York.
But Wolsey was too much engrossed in his am-
bitious political schemes to trouble himself much
about the obscure heretics of Buckinghamshire.
Besides, he only held the see for a few months,
and it may have been his successor, William
Atwater, whom White referred to. In any case,
the latter's hope was realised for the time. It
was not till Atwater died at Wooburn in 1520,
and was succeeded by John Longland, who had
been the King's confessor, that persecution recom-
menced in the county. The bowels of Bishop
Atwater, by the way, according to the strange
old custom of the time, were interred in Wooburn
Church, as were those of his predecessors Russell
and Smith, and of his successor Longland.

While these events had been taking place at
Amersham, the persecution of the Lollards had
continued in other parts of the country. From
1501 to 1519, according to Foxe, five or six persons suffered in Smithfield, seven at Coventry,
five in Kent, five in the eastern counties, two
at Salisbury, one (if not more) at Newbury, and
one woman at Chipping Sodbury. All these, it
must be remembered, were Lollards; it is not
till some years later that we come to the first
Protestant martyrs properly so called.

Two out of this list, both burned in 1518, call
for special notice, from their connection with
Buckinghamshire. These were Thomas Man,

burned in Smithfield, and Christopher Shoemaker, who suffered at Newbury.

Thomas Man had a remarkable and somewhat romantic career, though Foxe tells it in a very confused manner (iv. 208-213). He was cited for heresy before Bishop Smith at Oxford (1511), and after a period of imprisonment, he recanted in St. Mary's, did open penance, and was kept as a kind of servant, with a faggot embroidered on his sleeve, first at Osney Abbey, and then at St. Frideswide's Priory. The charges against him included the holding of some strange mystical views about the true sacrament of the altar being in heaven. He had called the priests' pulpits "lying-stools," and had said that "holy men of his sect were the true Church of God, and the only true priests." After a while he escaped from Oxford into the eastern counties, and for several years led a wandering life. It is impossible to tell whether some of the journeys mentioned were before or after the abjuration at Oxford; but we trace him in London, at Stratford, Chelmsford, and Billericay in Essex, and in Suffolk and Norfolk. Then he seems to have come westward again, after a narrow escape of arrest at Colchester. We find him at Uxbridge, at Burnham (Bucks.), at Henley-on-Thames, and at last at Newbury. Here he found "a glorious and sweet society of faithful favourers, who had continued the space of fifteen years together, till at last, by a certain lewd person whom they trusted and made of their counsel, they were

bewrayed, and then many of them, to the number
of six or seven score, were abjured, and three or
four burnt." No trace of this holocaust is to be
found except in this isolated reference (iv. 213).
But elsewhere (iv. 217) we are told of one Christopher Shoemaker, a native of Great Missenden,
who met with a fiery death at Newbury in 1518.
He was charged with having read to Joan Say,
of Little Missenden, "out of a little book, the
words which Christ spake to His disciples," and
with having spoken against pilgrimages, image-
worship, and transubstantiation.

On leaving Newbury, Man made his way to
the neighbourhood of Windsor, where he heard
that there was "a godly and a great company"
at Amersham, to which he betook himself, and
where he became a trusted teacher, being known
as "Doctor Man." In all his wanderings, while
working for his daily bread, Man was diligent in
the spread of his principles, and thanked God
that he had made seven hundred converts. He
also assisted several persons to escape from Amersham, and the neighbourhood to the eastern
counties, where he considered that there would
be greater safety for them. One of these may
have been Henry Miller, who had come to Amersham from Kent, where he had abjured and done
penance. At Amersham, he worked as a wire-
drawer, "taught many heresies," and after a
while fled to Chelmsford (iv. 228). The time
came when Man had to flee also. He seems to
have found shelter for a time in the house of

Andrew Randal of Rickmansworth (iv. 226). In February, 1518, he was apprehended and brought before Dr. Hed, Chancellor of the diocese of London. It was asserted that he again recanted; but this seems doubtful. On March 29th he was delivered to the secular power, with the usual hypocritical request that he might not be put to death; but before noon of the next day, he was committed to the flames in Smithfield. There seem hopeless confusions as to dates in Foxe's narrative; but some of these, perhaps, may be due to the fact casually mentioned (iv. 234) that there was at Amersham "another Thomas Man," probably a permanent resident; and most likely it was to the house of this latter that the visitors before mentioned from London and Harrow were accustomed to resort. One of the two was charged with joining with the martyr Robert Cosin in dissuading Joan Norman from pilgrimages, image-worship, fasting communion, and auricular confession. "Also when she had vowed a piece of silver to a saint for the health of a child, they (Thomas Man and Robert Cosin) dissuaded her from the same" (iv. 214). This must have been not later than 1506.

CHAPTER XI

WE have now reached the year 1521, when John
Longland, Bishop of Lincoln, instituted a strict
inquiry into the prevalence of heresy at Amersham and elsewhere. The account of this, with
copious extracts from the register, occupies
nearly thirty pages of Stoughton's edition of Foxe
(iv. 217-246). It possesses a special interest
from the date. 1521 was the year in which Luther
stood before the Diet of Worms; and his views
were not only as yet but partially formulated,
but could only be known to very few in England.
We have here, therefore, the latest picture of
English Lollardy. A year or two more, and it
was greatly modified by Lutheran influences.
Foxe, with all his inaccuracies, had a keen per-
ception of the broad aspects of history. He shows
this when he points to these records as a complete
answer to the question, "Where was Protestantism before Luther?" and goes on to say :—

"Although public authority then lacked to
maintain the open preaching of the Gospel, yet the
secret multitude of professors was not much un-

equal : certes, the fervent zeal of those Christian
days seemed much superior to these our days and
times, as manifestly may appear by their sitting
up all night reading and hearing : also by their
expenses and charges in buying of books in English, of whom some gave five marks " (about £40
of present value), " some more, some less, for a
book. Some gave a load of hay for a few chapters
of St. James or of St. Paul in English . . . . .
To see their travails, their earnest seekings, their
burning zeal, their readings, their watchings,
their sweet assemblies, their love and concord,
their godly living, their faithful demeaning with
the faithful, may make us now, in these our days
of free profession, to blush for shame."

With express reference to the register here
cited by Foxe, Mr. Froude (*History*, i. 545, 546)
calls Longland " a wicked old man," " a person
in whom the spirit of humanity had been long
exorcised by the spirit of an ecclesiastic," and
describes him as " staggering along the last years
of a life against which his own register bears
dreadful witness." The Rev. A. R. Maddison,
F.S.A., in a paper published a few years ago by
the Lincoln Diocesan Architectural Society, seeks
to defend Longland from the charges brought
against him by Foxe, and repeated by Froude on
Foxe's authority. He says :—

" It is a remarkable fact that a vast number
of Foxe's references to Longland's Register cannot be verified. I can vouch for this, as I have
myself carefully gone through the memoranda,

which commence with the first year of Longland's episcopate, and end with the last."

Mr. Maddison suggests various explanations of the difficulty, as the existence of another register, now lost; that Foxe may have trusted to garbled extracts made by others—from what documents? it may be asked; and finally, the hypothesis of a deliberate forgery. The last conclusion appears to be that which he personally favours, for he goes on to say :—

" Had he not so persistently quoted Longland's Register at Lincoln as the source of his information, his stories would probably never have been discredited; but unfortunately the temptation to give an appearance of veracity has proved fatal to his purpose."

I fear that it must be said of Mr. Maddison that unfortunately the temptation to discredit an unpopular writer has led him to attach importance to the discovery of a mare's nest. If this " register " is a forgery, it is one of the cleverest the world has ever seen. Inimitably simple in its delineations of life and character, consistent in all its parts, full of minute local and family details, which, as we shall see, are capable of confirmation from all kinds of sources, it bears every mark of genineness. With all due respect to Foxe, I am sure that worthy and eloquent, but terribly rambling old writer could never have produced so complicated, yet so clear and consistent a document (though he has evidently interpolated remarks of his own here and there).

As regards the absence of any such document at
Lincoln, Mr. Maddison is not the first writer
who has called attention to it.   Dr. Churton, in
his *Founders of Brasenose* (p. 137, note) accounts
for it by saying that " Bonner had a famous commission from Queen Mary to search all registers,
and to take out of them everything inimical or
discreditable to Popery." But Bonner has quite
enough sins laid to his charge, without making
him responsible for the loss of this or any other
document.   The good Doctor fails to show how,
if Bonner had destroyed the register in the time
of Mary, Foxe could have " turned it over," as
he tells us that he did, in the time of Elizabeth.
It is more to the point that Foxe's quotations
from the extant registers of other dioceses are
found to be substantially correct.   Froude's
testimony on this point has already been cited.
We have seen, too, that it was possible for a
document to find its way from Lincoln to Oxford
in spite of Bishop Russell's anathema on any
one removing it from the diocesan registry.   I
also learn, by a courteous communication from
Mr. Maddison himself, that Matthew Parker,
when Dean of Lincoln, is known to have removed
many MSS. from Lincoln to Oxford.   On the
whole, it seems likely that the register may have
been the separate record of a special commission.

At least fifty surnames which occur in this document, and in another short one purporting to be
an extract from the Registers, are still locally
familiar, almost all in the same or adjoining

parishes, though often with a slight change in spelling. Africke (now Affleck), Andrew, Atkins, Bartlett, Bennet, Brown, Chapman, Chase, Clark, Cooper, Dean, Dell, Dosset, Fastendich (now Fassnidge), Frier, Garland, Gardiner, George, Gray, Grove, Harding, Hawes, Hawkes, Herne, Hill, Hoare, Hobbes, Jennings, Morden (now Morten), Nash, Norman, Page, Potter, Reve (now Reeves), Rogers, Saunders, Simons, Smith, Squire, Taylor, Timberlake, Treacher, Tredway, Ward, Webb, Wells, Weedon, White, and Wingrove, have all their representatives in the district to-day; and it is very curious, and characteristic of the strange separation which has always been noticeable between the Chiltern country and the Vale of Aylesbury, that scarcely any of these surnames occur in the long list of those prevalent in the county town, given by the late Mr. Gibbs, in his *History of Aylesbury*. That town is only sixteen miles from Amersham, yet there is no trace of Lollardy in its annals. The hill-country people, " the uplandish folk," were, and long continued, almost a race by themselves. There are names in the document, such as Gudgame, Milsent, Widmer, and others, which seem to have died out in the neighbourhood, but may still be traced, either in authentic documents, or in the names of farms formerly held by these families.

Applying another test, the parish registers of Amersham commence in 1562; and a very cursory examination of the first twelve years (in which

I am indebted to the courteous assistance of Mr.
J. Cheese) reveals the names of Barnard, Bennett,
Clark, Dormer, Dossett, Harding *alias* Harden,
Littlepage, Morton, Norman, Saunders, and
Tredway, all given by Foxe as belonging to resi-
dents at Amersham in 1521. It is even possible
that the Roger Bennett, whose wife Joan was
buried July 21st, 1567, and the Alice Tredway,
buried February 20th, 1564, might be the persons
of the same names who gave evidence before the
commission; but most of the names must be of
the next generation.

Again, in some extracts from the Amersham
churchwardens' accounts, given by Dr. F. G. Lee
in the *Records of Buckinghamshire* (vii. 43-51)
we recognise in 1530 and 1541 the names of
Robert Bartlett, John Gardiner, Henry, Thomas,
Edmund, and Roger Harding, and John Hill, as
well as the surnames of Barnard, Bennett,
Dormer, Dossett, Milsent, Saunders, Stamp,
Timberlake, and Tredway. There is thus cumu-
lative evidence that we are dealing with a veritable
historical document, not with a concoction of
Foxe's own.

CHAPTER XII

THE Bishops of Lincoln, in their visits to the southern part of their vast diocese, were accustomed to leave the Great North Road at Hatfield, and to pass along " the Bishops' Road " to Amersham, Wycombe, and Henley. It was along this road, most likely, that Bishop Longland passed in 1521. On arriving at Amersham, he commenced, according to Foxe's account, by examining on oath some of those who had abjured in 1506. These, " on pain of relapse," that is, of death, were compelled to denounce those who shared their belief, and as one after another was denounced, they also were summoned and examined, often repeatedly, the subjects of inquiry going back some twenty or thirty years, till the number of those suspected of heresy amounted to some two hundred. The proceedings seem to have lasted for several months, and give us a vivid idea of the methods of " the English Inquisition." Husbands, wives, parents, children, brothers and sisters, were forced to betray one another. The evidence implicated persons in the dioceses of London and Salisbury, as well as in that of

Lincoln; but two districts were specially affected. One was the Chiltern district in Buckinghamshire, around Amersham, Wycombe, and Beaconsfield, and including the Thames-side from Henley down to Staines. The other lay some miles to the west, in Berkshire and Oxfordshire, taking in both sides of the Thames, with the valley of the Kennet. The northern parts of Buckinghamshire and Oxfordshire are never mentioned. To a large extent, South Bucks was Lollard, but North Bucks remained devoutly Catholic; just as in the next century, the former took sides with the Parliament, and the latter with the King.

In these districts, it was found, there existed a community known as " the Justfast Men," or " the Known Men," who were believed to regard themselves as the only true Christians, and to marry only among themselves. The name of the " known men " was one of old standing among the Lollards. Seventy years earlier, Bishop Pecock tells us that the test question which one would put to another when he wished to learn if a third party was trustworthy, was, " Is he a known man?" He says that they used it in the sense of being " known of God "—" the Lord knoweth them that are His."

Longland came to Amersham, it appears, in person, and understanding that a family named Bartlet were among the most influential persons suspected of heresy, resolved to make an example of them. He summoned before him Robert and Richard Bartlet, well-to-do farmers, who, with

their brother John, had abjured and done penance
at Tylsworth's martyrdom. They were the sons
of old Richard Bartlet, of whom it was told that
one day, as he was threshing, a passer-by had
said to him, "God speed, Father Bartlet, ye
work sore." "Yea," answered the old man,
with a satirical reference to the doctrine of transubstantiation, "I thresh God Almighty out of
the straw." The old yeoman's wife Katharine
seldom went to church, pleading ill health, and
it was noted that when she did attend, she did
not join in the prayers, but "sat mum." As to
Robert Bartlet, we have seen that he was imprisoned at Ashridge in the College of the
Precious Blood about 1506. He was released
about 1513. Unable to rest in the doctrines of
Rome, he told his neighbour Alice Harding that
"he had thought to have called William Tylsworth false heretic, but now he was better
advised." Mistress Harding encouraged him to
stedfastness. "I am glad," said she, "that you
are converted to grace, and chosen to Almighty
God. Never forsake that you are called to; for
if you do, there is no hope left for you." Of
Richard she had said, "Here cometh a good man,
and I hope he will be a good man; but he hath so
much mind of buying and selling and taking of
farms that it putteth his mind from all goodness."

The Bishop's officer made his way to Robert
Bartlet's house, and summoned him to attend the
inquiry. His wife Isabel, standing "between the
threshold and the hall door," exclaimed in her

anguish, "Alas! now you are but an undone
man, and I but a dead woman!" The two
brothers, when examined, refused to criminate
themselves. On this the Bishop went to the
house of William Chedwell, another person who
had abjured, and who was now lying "sore sick
in his bed." He administered an oath to him
on the Gospels (these "known men" do not
seem to have shared the objection to oaths
expressed by some of the Lollards, as by those
burned at Coventry two years earlier than this);
and from him and several others he got sufficient
evidence to implicate the brothers. He also
examined their wives. From Richard's wife he
easily obtained what he required; but Isabel was
"somewhat more temperate of her tongue," and
tried her utmost to shield her husband. Robert
was called again. "Did you know your wife to
be of the sect of heretics before you married
her"? asked Longland. "Yea," answered Bartlet. "If she had not been of that sect, would
you then have married her?" "I would," he
replied; which seems to show that he at least
did not share the strict views on marriage
ascribed to the "Known Men." He had to
acknowledge that he had been conversant with
William Tylsworth, Thurstan Littlepage, and
Alexander Mastall. He had received the communion at Easter without confession, and he and
Littlepage between them had taught his sister
Agnes the Epistle of James. He and his brother
John (who was now probably dead) had attended

meetings addressed by the three leaders just
mentioned. "And if any came in among them
that were not of their side, then they would say
no more, but would keep all silence." He and
his brother Richard "detected" (be it remembered in dread of a fiery death) their own sister
Agnes Wells, as guilty of the four great crimes,
on which all these examinations mainly
turned :—

    (1). Reading the Scriptures in English.
    (2). Denying the bodily presence of Christ
         in the Eucharist.
    (3). Rejecting the worship of images.
    (4). Speaking against pilgrimages.

The sister herself was next questioned, and at
first refused to criminate any one else, but was
forced to do so by a rigorous cross-examination.
Isabel Bartlet, summoned again, was asked about
her exclamation at the hall-door. She tried to
explain it away, but in so doing the poor creature
contradicted her husband's evidence; and she
also " detected " several heretics both at Amersham and Hughenden. Ultimately the two
brothers and the sister had to do penance. Robert
Bartlet held two pieces of land at Amersham in
1541, as appears by the churchwardens' accounts.

    Another prominent family was that of the
Hardings, representatives of which, still mindful
of their Lollard descent, are to be found now
in Amersham and the neighbouring towns. The
" Old Meeting " or Upper Baptist Chapel was
built in the eighteenth century by members of

this family, and several of them are interred in
its little burying-ground. In 1506, Thomas
Harding and Alice his wife, Henry, Richard, and
Robert Harding had carried faggots up the hill
to Tylsworth's martyrdom, William, Roger, and
Edmund Harding were also suspected of heresy.
William and Roger had failed to appear when
summoned by the Bishop's Chancellor. Roger
" could not say his creed in Latin." But Thomas
and his wife were the most conspicuous of all.
Eslewhere (iv. 580) Foxe tells us that after doing
penance in 1506, they wore badges till 1515,
when Bishop Smith mitigated their penance, but
enjoined them to go once a year on pilgrimage
to Ashridge, to fast on bread and ale upon Corpus Christi Eve, and never to remove from the
parish of Amersham. During this inquiry, it
seems, Thomas was examined, but refused to
detect others. " In penance for his perjury,"
Longland ordered him to resume his badge,
wearing for the rest of his life a patch of green
cloth, embroidered like a faggot, before and behind. It is difficult to understand how he and
his wife escaped so lightly, as several witnesses
implicated them. Perhaps some of the evidence
referred to matters prior to the Great Abjuration ; but Thomas, as we shall see, was not to
meet his fiery death for eleven years longer. It
was certainly deposed that he and his wife did
not join in the prayers at church, and that many
" known men " resorted to their house after the
abjuration. Alice Harding was evidently a

woman of some energy and force of character. We have seen how she exhorted the brothers Bartlet; and Chedwell, the sick man, told how " when the priest was coming to Richard Bennet to give him the housel " (probably on his death-bed) Alice Harding " went before, and instructed him what he should do." Isabel Tracher, too, had put her daughter to service with Alice Harding, " because she could instruct her better than many others." The wives of Roger and William and the former's eldest daughter, also came under suspicion.

The Richard Bennet just now mentioned, with his brother Roger, had been among the faggot-bearers in 1506. Roger was now examined, and proved an important witness. He " detected " nearly thirty persons in Amersham and else-where. Several women, he said, on their way to and from church, " were wont to resort to one J. Collingworth's house, and there keep their conventicle." Mr. S. R. Pattison, by the way, in his *Religious Topography of England*, refers to this as " what appears to have been the first mention of a conventicle in English history;" but the word often occurs in fifteenth-century documents. This " J. Collingworth " was pro-bably the same as Joan Collingborne, who had been denounced to Bishop Smith by Alice Tred-way in 1511, for speaking against pilgrimages and image-worship. Bennet also mentioned that his own servant Thomas Gray, with John Jennings, James Morden's servant, and " George, servant to Thomas Tochel," had " carried about books in English." He himself had given or lent one of these books to John Butler, a carpenter, a leading " known man " at Uxbridge; and he was also acquainted with a woman at Henley, married to one David Lewis, who was the daughter of a man suspect of heresy. She had been heard to say, " The churchmen in old time did lead the people as the hen doth lead the chickens; but our priests do now lead the people to the devil."

The next witness was Thomas Rowland, apparently a man-servant. He was suspected on what seems a comically slight ground. He had once said, " If I lie, curse, storm, swear, chide, fight, or threat, then am I worthy to be beat; I pray you, good master of mine, if I offend in any of these seven, amend me with a good scouring." It was more to the purpose that he had been heard to say at another time to a friend, '' Ah, good Lord! where is all our good conversation that used to be among us when your master was alive?" Rowland said that he had seen Agnes Frank, William Frank's wife (who had been abjured before her marriage) " turn away her face from the cross, as it was carried about on Easter day in the morning of the resurrection." He knew, too, that old John Scrivener had " carried about books from one to another." Mr. Pattison, referring to this, speaks of Scrivener as " the first English colporteur on record;" but the reference is too vague to justify such a conclusion; besides, the charge was brought against others at the same time. Rowland also mentioned " J. Gardiner " who may have been the John Gardiner of Raans, mentioned in the Churchwarden's accounts in 1541.

James Morden next comes before us. He is described in one place as a " labourer ;" but if he were the same person who had a servant, John Jennings, in his employ, he cannot have been a labourer in the ordinary sense. The term was often very vaguely used ; and one remembers how, within the nineteenth century, that fine old relic of mediævalism, Bishop Philpotts of Exeter, cited a newspaper editor before him as a " labourer." Whatever his position, Morden had been abjured by Bishop Smith, who found that " he had used his Paternoster and Creed so much in English, that he had forgotten many words thereof in Latin." The Bishop bade him for the future to say them in Latin only, and enjoined on him a pilgrimage twice a year to Lincoln. After a year or two, Morden had substituted, without permission, a pilgrimage to Missenden, and had also been working six months out of the diocese, contrary to the injunction he had received not to leave it. He was now charged with this disobedience. The poor fellow confessed that he had " learnt his doctrine " of Thomas Chase, and of Agnes Ashford, of Chesham, to whom he had paid seven visits before he could learn by heart a few verses of the fifth chapter of Matthew. His sister Marian testified that he had taught her the Paternoster, Ave, and Creed, in English, and that he had persuaded her for the last six years not to go on pilgrimages or worship images. There were two brothers, Richard and Radulph, living at Chesham, and an uncle, John Morden, of Ashley Green, who were all suspected of heresy. James Morden, as we shall see, was ultimately burned, and his sister Marian abjured. Morten, as the name is now spelt, is a well-known name in the later annuls of Amersham Nonconformity.

Another witness, Thomas Halfeaker, who appears to have had no sympathy with the "known men," mentioned a number of persons as taking no part in the prayers when they attended service at Amersham Church; also others who had removed to a distance.

Thomas Holmes, who had borne a faggot in 1506, horrified the townsfolk by the wholesale manner in which he now betrayed his brethren, and they came to the conclusion that he must be "a fee'd man of the Bishop." He named nearly sixty persons, not only in Amersham, and in the neighbouring villages, but in various parts of Herts, Middlesex, and Oxfordshire.

One John Sawcoat mentioned Richard Sanders as "ever defending them that were suspected to be known men," and as having "bought out his penance, and carried his badge in his purse." His wife Alice Sanders, according to another witness, gave Thomas Holmes a shilling to buy a book for her daughter, when he told her that

a noble (6s. 8d.) would not suffice to buy it.
Another time she had contributed 6d. towards
the purchase of a book which cost no less than
five marks (£3 6s. 8d.)—a glimpse, by the way,
at the method by which expensive books were
sometimes obtained. Of course these sums must
be multiplied ten or twelve times to get at the
value at the present day. One thinks of this
couple as well-to-do, but somewhat stingy people
—the parents, perhaps, of the Thomas Sanders
who is mentioned in the churchwardens' accounts
as holding three pieces of land at Amersham
twenty years later. He seems to have then
resided at the " Bywyre " (Bury Farm?) There
was a man named Thomas Houre, who sometimes worked for Richard Sanders, and was " a
holy water clerk " at the church. He had been
supposed to lean to the views of the " known
men," but had afterwards given evidence against
them before Bishop Smith. On his coming back
one day from Wooburn, Mistress Sanders asked
him, " What news?" He replied that " many
were there condemned of heresy, and therefore
he would lean to that way no more." She immediately told him that " he would gain nothing
by it." He got no more work for her husband,
and not only so, but he lost his " holy-water
clerkship " (this looks as if some of the local
clergy must have had Lollard leanings, and one
of them, John Barber, was actually accused of
Lollardy). Houre came down in the world, and
probably considered himself a sort of martyr of

orthodoxy; but his old mistress commented on his downfall as a judgment for his informing, and held him up as a warning to others. A curious glimpse into the cross-currents of life in the little town.

Two persons of the name of John Scrivener, probably father and son, were examined. The younger was prevailed on to denounce a number of persons; but from the elder, the so-called "colporteur," very little could be elicited. It was no doubt the latter who had been abjured in 1506, and who was afterwards burned for relapse.

The William Littlepage, before mentioned as surviving till the reign of Elizabeth, was apprenticed to one of these Scriveners, who seem to have been blacksmiths. He had learned the Lord's Prayer and the "Hail Mary" in English from Thurstan Littlepage, who seems to have been his grandfather, the Creed from his grandmother, and the Ten Commandments from one John Frier. He and his brother John were now abjured.

Several witnesses had implicated John Morwin's wife, Isabel. She was examined, but without much result. Her sister, Elizabeth Copland, was then forced to appear against her. She stated that as they returned from a visit to their dying father, Isabel had said to her, "All who die pass either to hell or heaven," to which Elizabeth replied, "Nay, there is between them purgatory."

At another time, when Elizabeth had been on pilgrimage to the "Rood of Rest," the following conversation took place between the sisters :—

"If you knew as much as I have heard," said Isabel, "you would go no more on pilgrimage while you live; for all saints be in heaven."

"Wherefore then is pilgrimage ordained by doctors and priests?" asked Elizabeth.

"For gain and profit."

"Who hath taught you this, man or woman? Your curate, I dare say, never learned you so."

"My curate will never know so much; but if you will keep counsel, and not tell your husband, I will say more."

"I will not tell."

"But I will have you to swear."

Elizabeth would not do this, so the conversation went no further. Isabel Morwin was now abjured.

Emme Tylsworth, either widow or sister of the martyr, who had removed to Hawkswell, near Romford in Essex, was summoned, but proved an intractable witness. She would neither criminate herself nor others; and the Bishop ordered her, under pain of relapse, to "make certain faggots of cloth, and wear them on her upper garment, as long as she lived."

The case of Thomas Bernard, "husbandman," was a peculiarly sad one. He had been abjured in 1506, but had trained his children, Richard and Joan, in his views. Their evidence was now received against him, and probably sent him to the stake.

Many other Amersham folks gave evidence, and many more were suspected of heresy. We read of John Milsent, Thomas Dorman, Robert Andrew, John Hill, and John Dosset, who had all been abjured before. A man named Dorset or Dosset was landlord of the White Hart Inn a few years later. Thomas Dorman, " Yeoman Dorman," as he was called, was the uncle of a Catholic controversialist of Elizabeth's time, who became Foxe's bitter antagonist. Then there were William Grinder, who " could not say his creed in Latin;" William Rogers, perhaps the " Father Rogers " who had been imprisoned in the Little Ease, or more likely his son ; " Herne's wife " and " Widow Herne;" John Stamp and William Smith, " wheelers;" Alice Holting, who had dined before taking the sacrament on the plea of delicate health ; Joan Norman, a disciple of old Robert Cosin, and destined to share his fiery death ; William Trecher, who had " kept Thomas Grove in his house on Easter and Christmas Day, because he would not come to church ;" Isabel, his wife, who, in spite of her husband's rebukes, and though in good health, had refused to go to church upon holy days for the last three years ; Agnes Squire, who had boasted that she would never be ashamed of having been abjured for heresy ; and Roger Squire, perhaps her husband, who had been heard to mutter a curse on seeing one of the informers.

In the little hamlet of Woodrow, a mile out of the town on the Wycombe road, were two " known men," Thomas Cowper and Robert Stampe.   The later's wife used to attend the " conventicle " at Joan Collingworth's, and had neglected to perform the penance enjoined her by Bishop Smith.   Evidently a large proportion of the inhabitants of Amersham parish failed to come up to the standard of orthodoxy.   Not all, perhaps, of those who sympathised with the " justfast men " did so from the purest motives ; but a strong current of local sympathy was certainly running in their favour.

CHAPTER XIII

MORE OF THE JUSTFAST MEN

WHILE Amersham, as we have seen, was the centre and *rendezvous* of the Lollard remnant in this part of the country, we have abundant evidence that they were widely scattered throughout the surrounding parishes. In the town of Chesham, for example, three miles north of Amersham, there were several persons suspected of heresy. There was John Tracher (probably the same as the "John Cracher" mentioned as doing penance in 1506), who had taught Alice Brown the Beatitudes in English. There was Agnes Ashford, who, as we saw, had taught the same passage to James Morden. Agnes, we are told, had once been bidden to recite it before "six bishops" (a rather unlikely thing, unless she had been taken up to London), "who straightway enjoined and commanded her that she should teach those lessons no more to any man, and especially not to her children." This Agnes seems to have lived with her son, Richard Ashford, a blacksmith, at whose house she and some friends from Uxbridge once spent two hours reading in "a certain book of the Acts

of the Apostles in English." Thomas Tredway,
who seems to have been her son by a former
husband, had been taught by her not to worship
the images of the saints. Other suspected persons were Richard and Radulph Morden, the
brothers of James Morden of Amersham ; William
Norton ; Thomas Clement ; and Joan Grove, who
had instructed John Hill " in the Epistle of St.
James and other opinions."

The proceedings at Chesham were varied by
a case of witchcraft, which gives a vivid idea of
the superstition of the time. The wife of a man
named Sparke had lost some money, which had
evidently been stolen. Her husband sought the
counsel of two friars. They advised him to make
two balls of clay, and put them in water, enclo-
sing in them the names of the persons he suspected. " And so doing, the said Sparke came
to his money again." Probably the thief was
afraid to face the direful consequences which he
looked for from this piece of sympathetic magic.
The Bishop's court declined to proceed in this
matter. We get a glimpse, too, of a quarrel
between this same John Sparke and one Thomas
Hutton. Sparke had called Hutton a thief, and
was fined ten shillings by the magistrates ; but
Hutton, who had called Sparke " heretic," " paid
nothing."

In the little hamlet of Ashley Green,
on the Hertfordshire border, lived John
Morden, the uncle of James, Richard, and
Radulph, who had in his house a book of

the Gospels and "other chapters in English."

At Little Missenden, three miles from Amersham up the beautiful valley of the Misbourne, the Vicar himself was believed to be tainted with heresy.   So also were Elizabeth, the wife of Henry Hover; John Say, to whom the martyr Shoemaker had read Christ's words out of his "little book;" William Say, his son; two Edward Popes (father and son); John Nash; Henry Etkin and his mother; as well as Joan Clark (perhaps the unhappy daughter of William Tylsworth), who had said "she never did believe in the sacrament of the altar, nor ever would believe in it."

Two miles further up the Misbourne lies the village of Great Missenden, the abode of the martyrs Christopher Shoemaker and Robert Cosin.   Here heresy seems to have penetrated not only so near to the walls of the Abbey, but to the very shadow of St. Mary's shrine; for one of the Canons of the Abbey was accused of it, with what result does not appear.   Among the villagers, William Atkins, Richard Dell, and Alice Nash are mentioned as suspected.   The name of Dell occurs among the Bucks Quakers of the next century.   It is still familiar in the parish.

The little village of Hitchenden, well known under its modern name of Hughenden as the abode of Lord Beaconsfield, gave shelter to several Lollards at this time.   Their leader was John Phip, described as a physician, who had done penance in 1506.   He is said to have been "very ripe in the Scriptures," and had a valuable collection of books, which he burned when he found himself in danger. His neighbour Roger Parker told him that he was "foul to blame" for this, as they were worth a hundred marks (£600 or £700 of present value). "I had rather burn my books," sagely answered Phip, "than that my books should burn me." He was now called before the Bishop, but was so cautious in his replies that no relapse could be proved against him by his own evidence. All that could be elicited from him was a story about one Thomas Stilman, who, when imprisoned in the Lollards' Tower at St. Paul's, had managed to climb into the belfry, where he cut the bell-ropes, tied two of them together, let himself down into the churchyard, and so made his escape. Phip's sister Sybil, and her husband Thomas Africk (who lived somewhere in the county, but not at Hughenden), were also examined against him, but with no better results. This name survives in the district in the form Affleck, but the original spelling is preserved in Africk's Farm, Little Missenden. William Phip, another member of the family, testified that John had spoken against image-worship, and other witnesses had heard him read the Gospels and a treatise in English on the Lord's Prayer. His daughter, too, had been heard to say that "she was as well learned in all things as the parish priest, save only the saying of mass." But William Phip, with his daughter, and his son

Henry, were under suspicion too. William
had spoken to one Roger Dods about image-
worship, and then told him "it was good
to be merry and wise," meaning "he should
keep close that was told him, or else strait
punishment would follow." Roger said that
once, in 1515, he had asked young Henry Phip
whether he was going to Wycombe. Henry
had just been chosen "keeper of the rood-loft,"
and carelessly answered, "I must needs go and
tend a candle before my Block Almighty." It
does not very clearly appear from this whether
the crucifix he referred to was at Wycombe or
Hughenden. Mr. Parker (*History and Antiquities of Wycombe*, p. 136) says it was in the old
Guild Chapel of St. Mary. Henry was now
cited and compelled to own his words ; and both
he and John Phip afterwards abjured.

One little point in William Phip's evidence
ought not to be passed by without notice. He
stated that Thomas Africk, in asking for his
relations at Hughenden, enquired "How do my
cousin Widmore, and Clerk the elder, and John
Phip do at Hichenden? Do they keep the laws
of God, as they were wont?" Now this is a
way of speaking thoroughly characteristic of the
Lollards. In all the remains we have of them
the word "gospel" scarcely ever occurs, though
it was so constantly on the lips of the first Protestants a few years later. With the Lollards,
the Old and New Testaments were "the Old
and New Law." More than a hundred years

before, Knyghton tells us (col. 1664) that they
were constantly speaking of "Goddislawe," and
asserting that no one was acceptable to God who
did not keep it as they set it forth.

Africk's cousin Widmore (the name is also
spelt "Widemore" and "Wigmer") was a
farmer, living perhaps at the hamlet now called
Widmer End.   Thomas Widmore had married
another sister of John Phip, so that he was really
Africk's brother-in-law.   His son Thomas and
his wife also came under suspicion.   "Clerk the
elder" is Thomas Clerke, who, with his son of
the same name, is several times named.   To the
house of one of these Clerkes there came one
day a tinker from Wycombe, called Christopher,
with whom he had some vague discourse about
the "poverty" and "misgovernment" of the
times.   A week after, when the tinker came
again on his round, he asked Clerke "how his
last communication with him did please him?"
"Well," was Clerke's reply, "I know more,
and can tell you more," said Christopher.   "See
that you believe in God in heaven; for there
be many Gods on earth, and there is but one
God; and He was once here, and was ill dealt
with, and will come no more till the day of
doom."   He went on to say that "the sacrament
of the altar was a holy thing, but not the flesh
and blood of Christ that was born of the Virgin."
He begged him not to divulge his words to his
wife, whose brother was a priest.   Not
long after, the priest got his sister to buy

him some " singing bread " (sacramental wafers).
It was damp, and the priest was laying it out
to dry, when his brother-in-law ventured to
suggest, " If every one of these is a god, then
there are many gods." " Till the holy words
are spoken over it," said the priest, " it is of
no power ; and then it is very God, flesh and
blood ; but it is not meet for any layman to speak
of these things." The next time Christopher
came to Hughenden, Clerke told him of the talk
he had had with his brother-in-law, and asked his
opinion of the matter. The account closes with
the tinker's answer. " Let every man say what
they will, but you shall find it as I show you ;
and if you will take labour to come to my house,
I will show you further proof of it." Other
persons who had come under suspicion at
Hughenden were Roger Parker, who was now
dead ; Lawrence Herne ; the wife of Thomas
Potter, and three men named Hobbes or Hobs.

In the town of High Wycombe we read of no
accused persons except the tinker Christopher.
But at West Wycombe there was Elizabeth, the
wife of Richard Dean, who had sometimes
attended the " conventicle " at Amersham ; and
also William Hobbes, who had been denounced
as a heretic by his brother Radulph to Bishop
Smith, but had escaped at the intercession of the
parish priest. In connection with him we read
of Oliver Smith and his wife of " Newline "—
possibly Newland, adjoining the town of High
Wycombe. In the remote village of Hambleden,

almost at the south-west corner of the county,
John Horne, a carpenter, was believed to be a
" known man."

In the town of Marlow several persons were
suspected of disaffection to the church. Thomas
Rave, a rough fellow, something of the type of
Aylward, the Henley blacksmith of sixty years
before, had been cited before Bishop Smith, who
ordered him to do penance at Wycombe, and to
go on pilgrimage to Lincoln. At Wycombe, he
" bound his faggot with a silken lace," no doubt
out of bravado. On his way to Lincoln, he called
some other pilgrims whom he met returning from
the shrine of Sir John Shorne " fools and idola-
ters." Passing a ruined chapel, he sneered at
it as " a fair milk-house down;" and in the
cathedral itself he behaved with disgusting
indecency. Not the most creditable type of Lollard, it must be admitted.

Others detected at Marlow were John Gray
(whose name is still borne by a local Nonconformist family of old standing) ; " Ward's wife ;"
and also John Simons, or Symonds, and his wife
Matild. The latter couple deposed to a prediction
uttered in their house by a certain John Hacker
(the name is also spelt Hakker and Haggar).
This man, who lived in Coleman Street, London,
was mentioned by several witnesses, and seems
to have been one of the wandering Lollard
teachers. The priests, he said, would bear rule for
a time, but would then be put down, with their
" false gods." " And after that we shall know

more, and then shall be a merry world." The
people here would be in close touch with Henley,
that ancient seat of Lollardy, if not of Walden-
sianism, where nearly a dozen persons were now
" detected."

Wooburn, as the bishop's residence, was likely
to be well guarded against heresy. Yet even here
" the wife of John Scrivener, smith," a relation
perhaps of the Amersham Scriveners, was under
suspicion.

At Beaconsfield, Richard White and his son-
in-law Bennet Ward carried on the uncouth pro-
cesses of the old woollen manufacture, treading
or " walking " the cloth, bleaching it, and
teasing it with teasel-heads to raise a nap ; unless
indeed they had set up one of the fulling-mills
which were then looked on with dislike as a
new-fangled innovation.   Both of them came
under suspicion, and had to abjure.   Ward had
in his possession the Gospels of Matthew and
Mark, and the Ten Commandments in English.
He had sheltered one Thomas Pope in his house,
and his wife and daughter had been heard to say
that Pope was " the devoutest man that ever was
in their house, for he would sit reading in his
book till midnight many times."   One John
Marston testified that Ward had said, "It
booteth no man to pray to Our Lady, nor to any
saint or angel in heaven, but to God only, for
they have no power of man's soul."

In the adjoining parish of Penn, Edmund Hill
and John Frier are named.   Frier, who had

taught the lad William Littlepage the commandments in English, was a servant of the Penn
family, the original stock of the Wiltshire house
from which, in the next century, sprang the great
Admiral, and his son, the founder of Pennsyl-
vania.

In the flat district at the south of the county,
with its green meadows and elm-fringed lanes,
numerous persons were " detected." At Dorney,
the charge of heresy was laid against John Sche-
pard and Robert Rave, perhaps the " Father
Reive " who had been branded in 1506. For
words spoken not long after that against transubstantiation and image-worship, he was now
cited, and ultimately burned. One charge against
him was that, on hearing " a certain bell in an
uplandish steeple," the old man had said, " A
fair bell to hang about any cow's neck in this
town !"

At Chalvey one Matild Philby was accused.
At Horton Robert Freeman, the parish priest,
had been seen reading a suspicious-looking book,
which, on seeing himself observed, he closed and
took to his room. In the adjoining parish of Iver,
the priest appears in a less creditable light. The
wife of Richard Carder, a man who was cited
for heresy, confessed that her husband's suspi-
cions as to her relations with the vicar were too
well founded, and Longland forbade her entering
the vicarage in future. It would seem that one
Jenkin Butler had been cited for heresy from
this village. Carder asserted that the Bishop had

wronged Butler, and said that he would have
warned him had he known of his intended arrest.
He boasted that he was ready to face burning
for his views ; but his courage failed him when
it came to the test, and his name appears among
the list of those who recanted. A more conspicuous " known man " in this parish was Robert
Durdant, several times referred to as " Old Durdant of Iver Court." The family was an old
one in the district, and had held land in Denham
parish from 1259 to 1414. Robert seems to have
been a substantial yeoman-farmer, and had a son
Nicholas, living at Staines, and another, Davy,
at Ankerwyke. On one occasion, when his sons
and their wives had been dining with him, he
ordered a boy who was present to leave the room,
" that he should not hear and tell," and " did
recite certain places unto them out of the Epistles
of St. Paul and of the Gospels." At another
time, a number of friends were present at the
marriage of his daughter. After the wedding
they met in the barn, and heard an Epistle of
Paul read. Among the guests were some with
whom we have met before—Henry Miller, the
Kentish wire-drawer ; Mistress Barret, the goldsmith's wife from London ; and Isabel Harding.
They " well liked the reading, but especially
Durdant, and commended the same."

Iver Court was evidently a favourite resort of the
" known men." All one night in 1518, several
of them, from Uxbridge and the neighbourhood,
sat up there hearing " a great book of heresy,"

apparently Wycliffe's New Testament, read by
Richard Butler. Durdant implored them not to
divulge the fact of his possessing the book, '' lest
he should be burned for the same;'' but the
matter got abroad, and Butler and others were
cited before Fitzjames, the Bishop of London
(Foxe, iv. 178). A large number of persons were
now detected at Uxbridge. Some of these had
been among Colet's hearers at St. Paul's.

'' Old Durdant '' was once asked by a woman
who seems to have been in his employment,
'' Joan Cocks, the wife of Robert Wywood,'' (the
maiden name being retained as in the old Scottish custom), ''that he, being a known man,
would teach her some knowledge of God's law,''
which he appears to have done. Another glimpse
is given us of one John Clerke of Denham, who
was eager to learn from the '' known men '' of
Uxbridge and the neighbourhood. One of these,
Richard Vulford of Ruislip, came by one day just
as Clerke had made a weele (a sort of osier trap
for catching fish). '' Now you have made your
weele,'' asked Vulford, '' can the weele turn
again and make you?'' '' No,'' replied Clerke.
'' Even so hath God made all priests, as thou
hast made the weele,'' said Vulford ; '' and how
can they turn again and make God?''

A certain Robert Pope, who had fled from
Amersham at the time of the Great Abjuration,
and was now living at West Hendred in Berkshire, was examined by the court of inquiry. He
not only denounced a number of persons in Buc-

kinghamshire (including his own father Edward
Pope of Little Missenden) but a number of persons
in the district in which he was now living; and
this wholesale delation was confirmed by numerous witnesses, who "detected" numerous
persons at Newbury, Hungerford, Wantage,
Burford, Witney, and other places in Berkshire
and Oxfordshire.

The "known men" were largely poor and
ignorant folk; they shared in many of the faults
and errors of the time; but their faces were
towards the light, and it was in their lowly homes,
rather than in the palace or the cathedral, that
the promise and the potency of the coming change
really lay.

CHAPTER XIV

THE ARGUMENT OF FIRE AND FAGGOT

WE may conceive something of the anguish, the terror, and the shame, which must have been caused by the pitiless inquisition of Longland. Some fled rather than betray their loved ones; others, it it said, died of grief and remorse after giving evidence; and many lives must have been clouded ever afterwards. As the Bishop's " sumners " went to and fro among the villages and farms, they met with anything but a favourable reception, and it would seem even with forcible opposition in some cases. But Windsor was close at hand; and Longland obtained a letter from the King, which is given by Foxe as follows :—

" Henry the Eighth, by the grace of God King of England and of France, Lord of Ireland, Defender of the Faith; to all mayors, sheriffs, bailiffs and constables, and to all other our officers, ministers, and subjects, these our letters hearing or seeing, and to every of them, greeting. Forasmuch as the right reverend father in God, our trusty and well-beloved counsellor, the Bishop of Lincoln, hath now within his diocese no small

number of heretics, as it is thought, to his no
little discomfort and heaviness : we therefore,
being in will and mind safely to provide for the
said right reverend father in God and his officers,
that neither they nor any of them shall bodily
be hurt or damaged by any of the said heretics
or their fautors, in the executing of justice unto
the said heretics, according to the laws of Holy
Church, do straitly command you and every of
you, as ye tender our high displeasure, to be
aiding, helping, and assisting the said right reverend father in God and his said officers, in the
executing of justice in the premises, as they or
any of them shall require you so to do ; not failing
to accomplish our commandment and pleasure in
the premises, as ye intend to please us, and will
answer to the contrary at your uttermost perils.

" Given under our signet at our Castle of
Windsor, the twentieth day of October, the
thirteenth year of our reign, 1521."

A curious point arises here, supposing the date
to be correctly given. The bull by which Leo
X. conferred on Henry VIII. the title of
" Defender of the Faith " bears date Oct. 11th,
1521. A courier could scarcely have reached
Windsor from Rome in nine days ; but the King
may have received private information of the
intended despatch of the bull.

Some in the long list of persons detected were
now dead ; others had disappeared ; and some
may have satisfied the Bishop of their innocence
of the charges brought against them. But a

large number were abjured, being obliged to take an oath on the Gospels that they "did utterly and voluntarily renounce, detest, and forsake, and never should hold hereafter these or any like opinions, contrary to the determination of the holy mother church of Rome; and further, that they should detect unto their ordinary whomsoever they should see or suspect hereafter to teach, hold, or maintain the same."

Foxe's account, now that he is no longer following a document, becomes confused again. He gives a list of forty-two men and eight women who recanted, but implies that the list is not complete. Some, he says, were condemned to perpetual penance in various monasteries, at Ashridge and Notley in Buckinghamshire, at Abingdon in Berkshire, at St. Frideswide's, Osney, Thame, Bicester, and Eynsham in Oxfordshire. Here, it seems, they were kept in a kind of slavery, and never allowed to pass the precincts of the monasteries. Others retained their liberty on condition of a humiliating penance, to be performed "under pain of relapse." The penance exactly corresponds with that prescribed in extant diocesan registers of the period. They were to go thrice round the market-place of some town, on a market-day, and then stand a quarter of an hour on the highest step of the market-cross, with faggots on their shoulders, to go before a solemn procession to the church on a Sunday, again carrying faggots, and kneel before the high altar all the high mass time. They were to repeat the same penance in their own parish churches, and once in a general procession elsewhere, and to bear a faggot, if required, at the burning of a heretic. Uxbridge, and Burford in Oxfordshire, were especially named as scenes of these melancholy processions. The penitents were also to fast every Friday on bread and ale, and on the eve of Corpus Christi upon bread and water. They were to repeat "Our Lady's Psalter" every Sunday and Friday during life. They were "never to haunt again together with any suspected person or persons, unless it were in the open market, fair, church, or common inn or alehouse, where other people might see their conversation." Lastly, it was ordered "that neither they, nor any of them, shall hide their mark upon their cheek, neither with hat, cap, hood, kerchief, napkin, or none otherwise, or shall suffer their beards to grow past fourteen days." It is not clear from this whether the cruel punishment of branding was revived at this time, or whether the reference is only to those who had been branded in 1506.

Foxe next gives the names of six persons who, having previously abjured, were now condemned for relapse, and handed over to the secular power to be burned. These are Thomas Bernard, James Morden, Robert Rave, John Scrivener, Thomas Holmes, and Joan Norman.

We have already seen reason for believing that this, and not either of the dates which Foxe gives elsewhere, was the real time of Bernard and Morden's death. With regard to Holmes (who, it will be remembered, had turned informer), and to Joan Norman, Foxe seems a little doubtful if the sentence was actually carried out. There can be no doubt, however, that John Scrivener suffered at this time, and with him "Father" Rave of Dorney. Foxe elsewhere asserts (iii. 398) that Longland was present in person, and preached a violent sermon before the stake, in which he declared that "whoever they were that did but move their lips in reading of the Scriptures in English were damned for ever." This seems scarcely credible; but Erasmus and others give us almost as glaring instances of the fanatical objection to a vernacular translation on the part of the clerics of the day.

There was a close adherence in the methods of the execution to the hideous precedents of Tylsworth's burning. There was the procession of faggot-bearers up the hill, and the same refinement of cruelty in forcing John Scrivener's children to set fire to their father's pyre, as in the case of Tylsworth's daughter. But this time, as Fuller tells us in his *Church History*, the infamy was not allowed to pass without a vigorous protest. The clerical party, he says, defended the act by quoting Deut. xiii. 6-9; "If thy brother, the son of thy mother, or thy son, or thy daughter, or the wife of thy bosom, or thy friend, which is as thine own soul, entice thee secretly, saying, 'Let us go and worship other gods,' . . . . . thou shalt surely kill him; thine hand shall be first upon him to put him to death, and then the hand of all the people." But, as Fuller points out, nothing is said of father or mother here; while even by the laws of pagan Rome the evidence of the child could not be received against the parent.

CHAPTER XV

LOLLARDY PASSING INTO PROTESTANTISM

AFTER the death of the Amersham martyrs in 1521, a period of comparative freedom from persecution ensued throughout England. One man suffered at Coventry the same year; but after this no other seems to have endured the " trial of fire and faggot " until 1530.

In the meanwhile the face of affairs was being wholly changed. While Henry was warring with France, and Wolsey was taxing the country to the utmost limit of endurance, and intriguing for the Papal tiara, the writings of Luther and his fellow-reformers were being brought into England, and Tyndale was translating the New Testament at Cologne and Worms, and afterwards part of the Old at Antwerp. The vigilance of the authorities proved all in vain to hinder the circulation of the forbidden book. The parchment scroll of the Lollard was gradually being superseded by the quaint black-letter volume of the Gospeller, with its more modernised version. The better day for which the Lollards had long been looking, and the coming of which some of them had vaguely predicted, seemed to be dawning at last. A strong reforming party was arising among the clergy, and was to some extent favoured by Archbishop Warham.

In nothing was the change in affairs more noticeable than in the neglected condition of the religious houses. Men had grown tired of endowing monks who were despised as lazy, and often believed to be immoral. The church-tower rose in all the beauty of the Perpendicular Gothic ; the priests ministered in gorgeous vestments, singing masses for the souls of pious donors who had bequeathed legacies for the purpose, and for lights to burn perpetually before the altar, for the repose of their souls. Meanwhile, in the ruinous buildings of the neighbouring priory, two or three monks were often all that remained of the goodly brotherhood of days gone by.

Of the religious houses in Buckinghamshire, since the alien priories were suppressed, those at Chetwode and Brill had been annexed to Notley Abbey during the Wars of the Roses. Luffield had been suppressed on account of its poverty in 1494. And now, in 1524, Ravenstone, Tickford, and Bradwell, having all become grievously decayed, were dissolved by a Papal Bull, and their revenues were given to Wolsey in aid of his great foundation of Cardinal College (now Christchurch) in Oxford. Of Bradwell we read that the buildings were " in decay for lack of pointing, tiling, walling, and thatching," and " the chancel roof of very evil timber." The fish-ponds, it is added, " now be wasted and little or no fish therein :" and while the Commissioners reported that the chancel and aisles might be repaired, they added, " and right necessary is it shortly to be done, for the salvation of the tile and timber." (Dugdale, *Monasticon*, iv. 510).

Wolsey's principal agent in the suppression of these priories was the man who was to give the death-blow to the old monastic system in England—the *Malleus Monachorum*, Thomas Cromwell. In 1527 the question of the divorce from Queen Catharine was raised. In 1529 came the fall of Wolsey, and in the following year his death. In 1531 Henry cast the die, and declared himself " Supreme Head of the Church of England." The casting off of the Papal supremacy had largely realised the political portion of Wycliffe's aims ; but Henry was as little as ever disposed to abandon the main features of Romanist doctrine, and after Wolsey's fall the policy of persecution was resumed as bitterly as before.

An extract given by Foxe (iv. 584) from the Lincoln Register of 1530 gives an interesting glimpse of the manner in which Lollardy was passing into Protestantism. A little company had gathered in the house of John Taylor of Hughenden, to hear a preacher from London, one Nicholas Field, who had been in Germany, and could tell them something of the new Reformers. It was probably by night, but some of those present had come for miles across the country. There were Thomas Hawks, and Thomas Clerk the younger, of Hughenden ; Robert Hawes and

Richard Dean, of West Wycombe; Thomas
Hern, of "Cobshill" (Coleshill?); William
Hawks, of Chesham; William Wingrave,
and others. Of these, Thomas Clerk and
the wife of Richard Dean had been under suspicion in 1521. Field read a portion of Scripture,
probably out of Tyndale's version, of which the
New Testament had reached England in 1526.
Perhaps some of the company had never seen a
printed Bible before. Then he addressed them,
telling them that "they that went on pilgrimages
were accursed," and that "it booted not to pray
to images, for they were but stocks made of
wood, and could not help a man." He denounced
saints' days, and also fasting days, without which
he found that they got on very well "beyond
the sea in Almany." It is curious to note that
he made an exception in favour of fasting on the
"Imbring" (Ember) Days. He spoke next of
the uselessness of offerings. One of the company
objected that "they maintained God's service."
"Nay," said Nicholas, "they maintain great
houses as abbeys and the like." He went on to
speak against Latin prayers, and recited the
Lord's Prayer, the Hail Mary, and the Creed in
English; after which he proceeded to denounce
the doctrine of transubstantiation. One of those
present probably betrayed the others, for all of
them, including Field, were "examined, excommunicated, and abjured" (not "burned," as Mr.
Pattison, by an odd blunder, asserts in his *Religious Topography*). The sweeping persecutions

of nine years before had evidently been far from extinguishing the remains of Lollardy in the district.

Another interesting case (Foxe, iv. 583) is that of a young man named John Ryburn, living at "Roshborough" (Risborough). He had met with a priest named Thomas Lound, who had spent two years at Wittenberg, and who was afterwards cast into the Fleet Prison in London. Ryburn had eargerly adopted the reformed doctrines, but his family were still devoted to those of Rome. His sister Elizabeth, coming to him on the eve of the Assumption, found him at supper "with butter and eggs," and was horrified at his inviting her to join him. "God never made such fasting days," said John; "but you are so far *in limbo patrum* that you can never turn again." At another time she spoke of going on pilgrimage to the Holy Rood of Wendover. "You do wrong," said John; "for there is never a step that you set in going on pilgrimage but you go to the devil; and you go to church to worship what the priest doth hold above his head, which is but bread, and if you cast it to the mouse, he will eat it; and never will I believe that the priest hath power to make his Lord." He admitted that he kneeled down at the elevation of the host, but said "he had no devotion nor believed in the sacrament." "The priests do naught," said he, "for they should say their service in English, that every man may know it, for if we had our Paternoster in English, we would say it nine times against one now." He had firmly grasped the doctrine of justification by faith, on which the Lollard view had been somewhat vague. "The blood of our Lord Jesus Christ," he said, "hath made satisfaction for all ill deeds that are done or shall be done; and therefore it is no need to go on pilgrimage." "The Pope's authority and pardon cannot help man's soul, and it is but cast-away money that is given for pardon, for if we ask pardon of our Lord Jesus Christ, He will give us pardon every day." At another time John was with his sister Alice "in a field called Brimmer's Close," a name which is still preserved in the parish of Prince's Risborough, where we have Brimmer's Farm and Brimmer's Hill, not far from Whiteleaf Cross. "A time shall come," he said to her, "when no elevation shall be made." "And what service shall we have then?" she asked. "That service," replied John, "that we have now." He was also charged with "having Jesus' Gospel in English," and with having been present in John Taylor's house at Hughenden, when one John Simonds "read to them a lecture out of the Gospel, of the passion of Christ, the space of two hours." This may have been the John Simons, of Marlow, accused in 1521.

Ryburn's two sisters, his father, and even his wife, were called before Bishop Longland, and compelled to depose against the outspoken Gospeller. It gives us a sad idea of the domestic divisions of the times. "A man's foes" were

indeed " they of his own household." Ryburn's
father also " detected " John Eaton of Speen,
and Cicely his wife, who " were marked of certain in the parish, on the Sunday last past, in
the sacring time, to hold down their heads, and
that they would not look upon the sacrament."
They had also been heard—heinous offence!—to
say, " What a clampering of bells is here!" as
they stood in a butcher's shop while the bells
were ringing for Holy Cross Day.

John Simonds, the reader just now mentioned,
was himself cited. He gloried in having " converted eight priests to his doctrines, and holpen
two or three friars out of their orders." He was
charged with defending the marriage of the clergy,
and also with saying, " Men do walk all day in
purgatory in this world, and when they depart
out of this world, there are but two ways, either
to hell or heaven."

Under the next year (1531) we find a curious
passage in the first edition of Foxe (ed. 1563,
page 490). It may best be given in the quaint
original spelling :—

" The Storie of a certaine olde man of Buckingham Shyre.

" I have found in a certaine place mention to
be made of a certaine olde man, which for eatyng
of Bacon in the Lent (dwelling in the countie of
Buckingham) was condempned to the fyre and
burned, in this yeare of our Lord 1531. As
touching his name and other circumstances which
perteine unto the true setting fourth of the his-

tories, we cannot fynde or understande any more. Notwithstandyng I have thought good not to pass over this matter with silence, for the memoriall of the man hymselfe, albeit I know not his name.''

This paragraph is omitted in the later editions. Whether Foxe found it erroneous, or whether he left it out to make room for more important matter, can only be conjectured. The violation of fasting days was not an infrequent ground of prosecutions for heresy, but it could scarcely have brought a man to the stake.

CHAPTER XVI

THE LAST OF THE LOLLARD MARTYRS

ONE of those who had had to do penance at Amersham, both in 1506 and in 1521, was Thomas Harding. In 1532, the date at which we have now arrived, he was an aged man; and his outspoken wife Alice was probably dead by this time. He continued to wear the green badge enjoined him in 1521, but he seems to have been allowed to remove from Amersham to the adjoining parish of Chesham, where a farm called Dungrove is pointed out by local tradition as his abode. It is important to note that the account now about to be quoted from Foxe does not purport to be quoted from the Diocesan Register, but "from the written testimony of certain inhabitants of Amersham." Foxe says :—

"At last the said Harding, in the year above said (1532), about the Easter holidays, when the other people went to church to commit their wonted idolatry, took his way into the woods, there solitarily to worship the true living God in spirit and in truth; where, as he was occupied with a book of English prayers, leaning or sitting upon a stile by the wood's side, it chanced that

one did espy him where he was, and came in
great haste to the officers of the town, declaring
that he had seen Harding in the woods looking
on a book; whereupon a rude rabble of them,
like mad men, ran desperately to his house to
search for books, and in searching went so nigh
that under the boards of his floor they found certain English books of Holy Scripture. Hereupon
this godly father, with his books, was brought
before John Longland, Bishop of Lincoln, then
lying at Woburn, who, with his chaplains, calling
Father Harding to examination, began to reason
with him, proceeding rather with checks and
rebukes than with any sound arguments. Thomas
Harding, seeing their folly and rude behaviour,
gave them but few words, but fixing his trust
and care in the Lord, did let them say what they
would. Thus at last they sent him to the
Bishop's prison, called Little-ease, where he did
lie with hunger and pain enough for a certain
space, till at length the Bishop, sitting on his
tribunal seat like a potestate, condemned him for
relapse to be burned to ashes, committing the
charge and oversight of his martyrdom to Rowland Messenger, vicar of Great Wycombe. This
Rowland, at the day appointed, with a rabble
of others like to himself, brought Father Harding
to Chesham again, where, the next day after his
return, the said Rowland made a sermon in Chesham Church, causing Thomas Harding to stand
before him all the preaching time; which sermon
was nothing else but the maintaining of the

jurisdiction of the Bishop of Rome and the state
of his apostolical see, with the idolatry, fantsies,
and tradition belonging unto the same.   When
the sermon was ended, Rowland took him up to
the high altar, and asked him whether he believed
that in the bread, after the consecration, there
remained any other substance than the substance
of Christ's natural body, born of the Virgin Mary?
To this Thomas Harding answered, ' The articles of our belief do teach us that our Saviour
Jesus Christ was born of the Virgin Mary, and
that He suffered death under Pilate, and rose
from death the third day ; that He then ascended
into heaven, and sitteth on the right hand of
God, in the glory of the Father.'

" Then was he brought into a man's house in
the town, where he remained all night in prayer
and godly meditations.   So the next morning
came the aforesaid Rowland again, about ten
o'clock, with a company of bills and staves, to
lead this godly father to his burning ; whom a
great number both of men and women did follow,
of whom many bewailed his death, and contrary,
the wicked rejoiced thereat.   He was brought
forth, having thrust into his hands a little cross
of wood, but no idol upon it.   Then he was
chained unto the stake, and desiring the people
to pray for him, and forgiving all his enemies
and persecutors he commended his spirit to God,
and took his death most patiently and quietly,
lifting up his hands to heaven, and saying, ' Jesus,
receive my spirit.'

"When they had set fire on him, there was one that threw a billet at him, and dashed out his brains; for what purpose he so did it is not known, but, as it was supposed, that he might have forty days of pardon, as the proclamation was made at the burning of William Tylsworth above mentioned, where proclamation was made the same time that whosoever did bring a faggot or a stake to the burning of a heretic should have forty days of pardon; whereby many ignorant people caused their children to bear billets and faggots to their burning.

"In fine, when the sacrifice and burnt-offering of this godly martyr was finished, and he burnt to ashes in the dell going to Botley, at the north end of the town of Chesham, Rowland, their ruler of the roast, commanding silence, and thinking to send the people away with an *Ite missa est*, with a loud voice said to the people these words, not advising belike what his tongue did speak, ' Good people! when ye come home do not say that you have been at the burning of a heretic, but of a true Christian man ;' and so they departed to dinner, Rowland, with the rabble of other priests, much rejoicing at the burning of this good man. After dinner they went to church to evensong, because it was Corpus Christi even, where they fell to singing and chanting, with ringing and piping of the organs. Well was he that could reach the highest note, so much did they rejoice at this good man's burning. He should have been burned on the Ascension even, but the matter was deferred unto the even of Corpus Christi, because they would honour their ' bready Messias ' with a bloody sacrifice. Thus Thomas Harding was consumed to ashes, he being of the age of sixty years and above."

The Rev. A. R. Maddison, in the paper on " Longland's Register " already referred to, says :—

" The register contains an account of Harding's examination, but it was conducted, not by the Bishop, but by his Vicar-General, John Rayne, assisted by Robert, Abbot of Thame and Suffragan Bishop, and Thomas Waterhouse, Rector of Ashridge. This commission found Harding to be guilty of re· lapse into heresy ; but Foxe does not mention an additional circumstance of some interest. According to the register, Harding craved for the benefit of absolution, and thereupon Rayne, the Vicar-General, pronounced him free from the greater excommunication, and restored to the bosom of the church. Again, the certificate sent to the King, setting forth Harding as a relapsed heretic, states that he had confessed his heresy before Bishop Longland at the Old Temple, London, not at Wooburn, as Foxe asserts. This took place on the 6th April, but the fuller examination before Rayne and his assessors was on the 29th May. Plainly, then, Foxe is not in harmony with his authorities, ... and his omission of Harding's recantation renders one suspicious of his trustworthiness."

Considering that Foxe's authority was *not* the Register, but the statements of the Amersham folks, the discrepancies cannot be said to be of much importance, or to throw discredit, as Mr. Maddison seems to think they do, on Foxe's references to the registers elsewhere. The inaccuracies as to date and place are just what might be expected after the lapse of forty years; and it is perfectly natural that Harding's neighbours should have slurred over the fact of that recantation, which, if it lessens his glory, throws into clearer relief the injustice and inhumanity of the authorities, when his memory had come to be surrounded with a sort of halo of saintship among them. It may even be that the recantation affords the real explanation of Messenger's supposed blunder in addressing the crowd.

This Rowland Messenger had been Vicar of High Wycombe since 1511, and it was by him that the beautiful tower of All Saints' Church in that town, " the cathedral of Bucks," was erected in 1522. He was also Cardinal Wolsey's clerk of the works at the erection of the great tower of Christ Church, Oxford. It is not likely that either he and his clerical friends, in the midst of the rejoicings Foxe describes, or Harding's old neighbours, as they made their way home to Amersham across the furze-clad common of Chesham Bois, and through the beech-woods in all their summer splendour, called to mind the fact that the persecution of the Lollards had now lasted exactly a century and a half. For it was

on Corpus Christi Day, 1382, that Philip Repyng-
don preached the sermon at Oxford which led
Archbishop Courtenay to take the first repressive
measures against Lollardy. And in a certain
sense, the story of that persecution ends with the
burning of Harding, who may fairly be called
the last of the English Lollard martyrs—the last,
that is, of purely Lollard training and sympathies.
Not only so, but with one exception (that of
John Frith, who was burned in Smithfield in
1533) he was the last who suffered under the *ex
officio* power of the bishops.

The spot of Harding's martyrdom is still
pointed out at Chesham, in a small chalk-pit,
not far from the police-station. When I saw it
a few years ago, it was fenced in, and occupied
by some very prosaic-looking sheds. On the hill
to the south of the town is a stile, leading into
a wood called Hodge Wood, which is said to mark
the site of that which Harding sat to
read. Little of the town can be seen
from this spot, except the church tower,
so that the view may be practically identical with
that on which the martyr's eyes then rested. An
old house which formerly stood near the Broad-
way at Chesham, lying back a little from the
road, and with a brook or ditch in front of it,
was pointed out as that in which he spent the
last night of his life. The house was pulled
down about 1870, and the site is now occupied
by a brush factory. In some articles on local
history, by Mr. R. S. Downs, which appeared

in the *Chesham Examiner* a few years ago, a tradition was mentioned to the effect that Harding was also confined for a time in the "parvise" over the church porch. Another tradition, it must be said a very absurd one, tells how, as Harding was being led up the hill, he hesitated whether he would not recant after all, and uttered the words, "Shall I mount?" whence, we are told, the hill derived the name of "Shally Mount," by which it is sometimes known. This is just one of those philological guesses by which local names are often accounted for, and is inconsistent with the facts brought to light by Mr. Maddison.

A local authoress, the late Miss Werry, published about forty years ago, a book called *Memorials of Agmondesham and Chesham Leycester; or, Two Martyr Stories*. Though written in a charming style, these "Memorials" have no pretensions to historical accuracy, and it is to be feared that they have tended to confuse the traditional accounts of the district. The first story, "The Schoolmaster of Agmondesham," contains incidents culled from various narratives in Foxe, especially his account of Thomas Benet, burned at Exeter in 1531. These are located at Amersham, and allotted to an imaginary William Chase. The second narrative, "A Memorial of Chesham Leycester," gives a somewhat distorted version of the trial and death of Thomas, or, as he is here called, John Harding. An interesting article on Harding's death appeared in the *Quiver* for May, 1888, under the title, " A Bucks Martyr Site and its Story." It was from the pen of the late Mr. W. J. Lacey (to whose courtesy I am indebted for some of the facts in this chapter), and was accompanied by excellent engravings of the site of Harding's death, and the view form " the martyr's stile."

Another trace of the martyr times, till lately existing near Chesham, may here be mentioned. Between Chesham and Latimer, lies an ancient building known as Blackwell Hall, possibly an old religious house. Here, according to an interesting article in the *Records of Buckinghamshire* (iii. 66, 67), human bones have been dug up in the garden, as well as several gold coins. On the walls of the kitchen might formerly be traced rude drawings of men and women chained to stakes and nailed to crosses; and on each side of the fire-place were texts of Scripture, which appear to be citations from Coverdale's version, given from memory. On the left, " Receive the word of God, wherewith ye may learn to know God ; happy are they that hear the word of God " (Jas. i. 21 ; Luke xi. 28). On the right, " He that is of God heareth God's words ; ye therefore hear them not, because ye are not of God " (John viii. 47). " Why do ye not understand my speech? even because ye cannot abide the hearing of my word " (John viii. 43).

CHAPTER XVII

THE TURN OF THE TIDE

A GREAT change in the relation of the State to the Church is manifest when we come to the year 1534, the year of the Act of Supremacy, and of the formal separation from Rome. In the same year it was enacted that a heretic, instead of being left to the arbitiary control of the episcopal courts, must be proceeded against by two witnesses in open court and tried by jury, with the right of admission to bail; nor could he be burned without a royal writ. '' The poisoned chalice '' which the Papal party had mingled for the Lollards was now commended to their own lips. In 1535, Sir Thomas More, Fisher, Bishop of Rochester, and others, were executed for refusing to take the Oath of Supremacy. It was no longer possible for zealots like Rowland Messenger to preach '' the maintaining of the jurisdiction of the Bishop of Rome, and the state of his apostolical see ;'' for no priest could preach without a license, and then, under heavy penalties, he was bound to maintain Royal Supremacy.

In the same year (1535) fourteen Dutch Anabap-

tists, who had come over to England, were burned,
two in Smithfield, the remainder in various towns.
Their execution was partly due to political
reasons. The excesses of John of Leyden and
Knipperdoling had made the name of Anabaptist
as much dreaded and hated as that of Anarchist
is to-day. Yet these poor unnamed Hollanders,
" who by no terror of stake or torture could be
tempted to say that they believed what they did
not believe," were, as Mr. Froude has said,
" assisting to pay the purchase-money for English freedom." And from this time the Anabap-
tists are often met with in English religious
history; and it is noteworthy that at a synod of
their leaders held in Westphalia in 1536, deputies
from England were present. There was every
likelihood that some of the Lollards would join
the new sect, whose more moderate leaders held
views very similar to their own. And this may
account for the fact that in some of the districts
where Lollardy had been strongest, and notably
in South Bucks, we find Baptists numerous in
the next century.

The right of Englishmen to have the Bible in
their own tongue, for which the Lollards had
so long contended, was won by slow degrees.
Tyndale's translation had been condemned for its
alleged inaccuracy, though amply vindicated by
the verdict of later ages. In 1530, Henry
promised to have the New Testament translated,
" to the intent he might have it in his hands
ready to be given to his people, as he might see

their manners and behaviour meet, apt, and convenient to receive the same."   But the Bishops
were divided on the matter.   Gardiner had a
preposterous scheme for a version in a medley of
Latin and English.   Cranmer petulantly wrote
that he saw no prospect of a version being agreed
upon " till a day after doomsday."   But in the
eventful year 1535, Miles Coverdale was able to
issue the Bible, under the patronage of Cromwell,
and in 1537 he published a second edition, " set
forth with the King's most gracious license."

Thomas Cromwell was now " vicegerent of the
King in all matters ecclesiastical;" stern, relent-
less, unpitying, and determined to humble the
Romanist party to the utmost.   Injunction after
injunction was issued to the clergy, for the abro-
gation of holy days, the discouragement of
pilgrimages and image-worship, and the teaching
of the Creed, the Paternoster, and the Ten Commandments in English.   Commissioners were
appointed to visit the religious houses, and
presented to Parliament their report, the famous
" Black Book."   Its revelations of the alleged
depravity of the monks were met by the Commons
with cries of " Down with them !"   The smaller
houses (all with incomes of less than £200 a
year) were now suppressed.   In Buckinghamshire this only affected Little Marlow,
where there were but two nuns, Medmenham, where there was a single monk,
and the house was entirely ruinous, and
Ankerwyke.   The revenues of all three were

annexed to the neighbouring abbey of Bisham in Berkshire.

But the Romanist party did not submit without resistance. On October 4th, 1537, as the beech-woods on the Chilterns were rich with their mellow autumn tints, three wearied horsemen, who had ridden day and night out of the far-off Fen country, came across the hills, bearing evil tidings to the King at Windsor. They were Heneage, one of the Royal commissioners, with Sir Marmaduke Constable and Sir Edward Madyson. The day before, at Horncastle in Lincolnshire, Heneage had been attacked by a fierce mob of people, led on by monks and priests. He had escaped from them, but the chancellor of Lincoln, who was with him, had been cruelly put to death. Bishop Longland had made himself as obnoxious to the Catholics by his Erastianism, as to the Gospellers by his persecution ; and his palace at Lincoln had been attacked and plundered. The summons to arms immediately went through the country ; and the men of Bucks and the other counties where " heretics " had most abounded, rallied to the support of the King. The Lincolnshire rising, and the still more serious revolt which followed in the North, the " Pilgrimage of Grace," were stamped out with ruthless severity. The nobles who had led the movement were sent to the block ; the abbots and squires to the gallows. And still the work of change went on. Images and relics were removed from their gorgeous shrines, and in many instances were brought to London to be burned. "Our Lady of Walsingham," "the Blood of Hales," "the Rood of Grace," were exposed to mockery and contempt, as mere juggles and impostures. But so violent a movement could not fail to bring about a reaction, and already there were ominous signs of a coming change. Henry and his advisers seemed nervously anxious to prove that they were not to be confounded with heretics; and in 1538 was witnessed the not very creditable spectacle of Cranmer and Thomas Cromwell assisting in the condemnation of John Lambert for views but little differing from their own.

In the same year, a man named Cowbridge, of a wealthy family in Essex, which had held Lollard views from the time of Wycliffe, was brought before the aged Bishop Longland at "a place beside Wickham" (no doubt at Wooburn), and charged with heresy. He had been living for some time at Wantage, where, as we have seen, Lollards were met with in 1521. Here, says Foxe (v. 252) he had "by a long season exercised the office of a priest in teaching and ministering of the sacraments, but being no priest indeed, and had converted many to the truth." Longland committed him to the Bocardo prison at Oxford, where he is said to have lost his reason, and he was burned in that city shortly after.

Mr. Maddison finds mention of this Cowbridge in the Longland Register, where it is stated that he had relapsed into heresy after solemnly abjuring it under Bishop Smith. He objects that no mention is made of his madness. Surely, if the authorities had acknowledged him to be mad, they would hardly have burned him! Here it must be noted that Foxe expressly says that he had *not seen* the account of Cowbridge's trial in the Register; and this may surely be regarded as a strong presumption that the register he quotes elsewhere is a different one from that examined by Mr. Maddison. Foxe was a student at Brasenose at the time of Cowbridge's death, and took his B.A. degree the same year. His account of this poor man must have been drawn from his own recollections, or from University gossip.

We now come to the fateful year 1539, the year of the final suppression of the monasteries, and of full liberty to read the Bible in English. The "greater abbeys," which had been left intact in 1536, were all dissolved, and their revenues confiscated. In Buckinghamshire the houses now suppressed were Ashridge (which became the nursery of the infant Prince Edward), Notley, Burnham, Missenden, Biddlesden, Snelshall, Lavendon, Ivinghoe, and the Friary at Aylesbury. The Grey Friars of Aylesbury were in debt; their revenues were only valued at £3 2s. 5d. per annum, and their chapel was meagrely adorned. They signed a document stating that they had "profoundly considered that the perfection of Christian living doth not consist in dumb ceremonies, wearing of a grey

coat, disguising ourself after strange fashions,
ducking and becking, in girding ourself with a
girdle full of knots, and other like Papistical ceremonies, wherein we have been most principally
practised and misled in times past; but the very
true way to please God, and to live a true Christian man, without all hypocrisy and dissimulation,
is sincerely declared unto us by our Master Christ,
His evangelists and apostles.'' A similar form
had to be signed by the friars in other parts of
England, e.g., at Leicester. It is satisfactory to
find that scarcely any of the Buckinghamshire
houses were charged with those revolting im-
moralities which were ascribed to some in other
parts of the country, though Longland himself
had severely censured some of the Missenden
canons not long before.

The inmates of the religious houses received
pensions for life. The Abbot of Biddlesden,
for instance, had £40, the sub-prior £6, and the
eight monks £5 6s. 8d. each. The Abbot of
Notley had what was then the large amount of
£100 a year, and lived to enjoy it till 1538.
Some pensions continued to be drawn when
James I. came to the throne. One of the canons
of Missenden became vicar of the parish, and
another, who had been accustomed to take services at Lee, received an addition to his pension
on undertaking to continue them. But great
distress was caused by the wholesale way in
which the dependents of the monasteries were
thrown out of employment. More than forty

persons, mostly agricultural labourers, thus suffered by the suppression of the nunnery at Burnham, which is admitted to have been well conducted. The new owner of the estate was put in bodily fear by the threats of the unemployed men. However desirable the suppression of the monasteries may have been from a religious point of view, it is impossible to speak too severely of the selfish and shameless greed with which it was carried out.

Some of the dispossessed abbots and monks embraced the Reformed doctrines. The Abbots of Missenden and Bisham both married, and the latter became a Protestant bishop.

In the same year (1539) the new edition of the Scriptures, the "Great Bible," was issued, and, by Royal authority, was placed at once in every parish church, while the clergy were bidden to "provoke, stir, and exhort" their people to read it. We can imagine the joy with which the Lollards would hail the newly-granted liberty, though this joy may have been damped by the discovery that the new version differed so much from their long-prized parchment scrolls. Strype says :—

"It was wonderful to see with what joy this book of God was received, not only among the learneder sort, and those that were noted for lovers of the Reformation, but generally all England over, among all the vulgar and common people; and with what greediness God's Word was read, and what resort to places where the reading of it was. Everybody that could bought the book, or busily read it, or got others to read it to them if they could not themselves, and divers more elderly people learned to read on purpose. And even little boys flocked among the rest to hear portions of the holy Scriptures read."

But while multitudes shared the Lollard desire for reading the Scriptures in English, many of them still dreaded the Lollard doctrine on the Eucharist. Alarmed by certain excesses on the part of the extreme Protestants, and anxious that his subjects should observe what he regarded as the golden mean between Roman superstition and Lutheran fanaticism, Henry had a Bill introduced into Parliament, styled with delightful simplicity " An Act for Abolishing Diversity of Opinions." This was the famous Statute of the Six Articles, or as the Protestants called it, " the Whip of Six Strings." It rendered penal the rejection of transubstantiation, of communion on one kind, vows of chastity, celibacy of the clergy, private masses, or auricular confession. Burning was the penalty for a denial of transubstantiation, and on a second offence, for an infraction of any of the other articles. Refusal to confess or to attend mass became a felony. Five hundred were indicted in London alone. Bishops Latimer and Shaxton were imprisoned; and Cranmer himself narrowly escaped.

In Longland's diocese, persecution broke out once more, but the charges were far less numerous and varied than those in 1521. In Buckinghamshire, William Fastendich, of Wooburn, and William Hart, of Great Brickhill, were charged with a denial of transubstantiation; the latter, who affords a solitary instance of a North Bucks heretic, having said, " Thinkest thou that God Almighty will abide over a knave priest's head?" Christopher Erles, of Risborough, was indicted for having looked down at his book instead of bowing at the elevation of the host. He had also been seen at work on a piece of fustian on a holy day, and when taxed with it had replied that "it was better to do that than to sit at the alehouse drinking drunk." William Garland, of West Wycombe, had said that extreme unction was a "godly sign," and not a sacrament. William Webb, of the same parish, had set "the image of a headless bear," most likely a broken piece of stonework, "in the tabernacle of St. Roke." Elenore Godfrey, of Great Marlow, was summoned for "laughing and speaking certain words against one Thomas Collard," whom she had characterised, it seems, as "a pope-holy hypocrite," and described him as "crouching behind the children in Marlow Church, and when the priest crossed his head with the ' saucer ' he would cross his head likewise." "For these words she was convented before the Bishop, and miserably vexed." (Foxe, v. 454).

Foxe here introduces the burning of James Morton (or Morden) and Thomas Bernard of Amersham; but we have already seen that this must have taken place at an earlier date. Next he speaks of one Barber, an Oxford M.A., who had been cited for heresy, and had defended himself with marked ability, but who recanted about this time, '' after which the good man long prospered not, but wore away.'' Was this person, here joined with two Amersham men, the '' John Barber, clerk, of Amersham,'' accused of heresy in 1521?

The closing years of the reign of Henry VIII. afford a most perplexing spectacle of confusion in religious affairs—Catholic and Protestant sympathisers among nobles and prelates intriguing and counter-intriguing at the Council-board; Catholic priests saying mass in one part of a church, while Protestant zealots were loudly reading the Scriptures in another; Catholics and Protestants dragged to Smithfield on the same hurdles, the first to be hanged for treason, the other to be burned for heresy. The Protestants of Bucks would hear at one time of a martyrdom on their own borders, when three Windsor men, Peerson, Filmer, and Testwood, were burned just below the Castle. A few weeks later they would hear how their accusers had been made to ride round the streets of Windsor, with their faces to the horses' tails, and papers on their heads charging them with perjury, and then had had to stand in the pillory. In the same year (1543) Jacob Mallet, a canon of Windsor, and formerly master of the hospital at High Wycombe, was executed for treason. The charge against him was that, speaking of the dissolution of the abbeys, he had said, "The King hath brought his hogs to a fine market!"

The Act of the Six Articles was considerably modified in 1546, and again in 1547. But on the other hand Henry complained that "that most precious jewel, the Word of God, was disputed, rhymed, sung, and jangled in every ale house and tavern;" and therefore he withdrew the liberty of Bible-reading from every one "under the degree of a gentleman," and prohibited Tyndale's and Coverdale's versions. This reign of confusion and compromise lasted till Henry's death in 1547. In the same year Bishop Longland passed to his account.

Edward VI. succeeded his father at the age of nine. A child whose playground had been among the deserted halls and walks of a Buckinghamshire monastery (the College at Ashridge) was not likely to have a very awful reverence for the old system; and his rapacious advisers had if possible even less. Sweeping changes were the order of the day. The Mass was changed into a Communion service. The marriage of the clergy was permitted. The churches were ruthlessly stripped of their adornments. Not only the Act of the Six Articles, but all the Acts passed against Lollardy in the reigns of Richard II., Henry IV., and Henry V., were repealed.

But the heart of the nation was far as yet from sanctioning the new reforms. In 1549 risings took place in Cornwall, Devon, Yorkshire, and Norfolk. They were due partly to

Romanist influence, and partly to agrarian dis-
content. A less important outbreak occurred in
Oxfordshire, in which many inhabitants of Bucks
(probably of the Catholic districts in the North)
were concerned. It was led by certain priests,
but was quickly suppressed by Lord Grey of
Wilton, who marched through the disturbed
region with a force of German mercenaries, and
hanged several priests on their own church towers.
A spirit of bitterness was being engendered,
which was preparing the way for a frightful reaction.

CHAPTER XVIII

In the spring of 1553 it became evident that the delicate, precocious boy-king was passing away. The Court removed to Greenwich, and the poor lonely little Edward was soon confined to the chamber of his last illness. On April 14th a remarkable incident took place at the Council table. John Knox, afterwards so famous in the history of the Scottish Reformation, was at this time in England, and had been appointed one of the King's chaplains. He had been offered first the see of Rochester, and then a living in London, but had declined, owing to conscientious scruples; and he was now summoned before the Council to state the grounds of his refusal. Having explained his objections to the polity of the English Church, he was courteously dismissed. As he had no objection to undertake itinerant work, he was asked shortly afterwards to go on a sort of preaching tour through Buckinghamshire. The following minute appears in the Council Register :—

"At Grenewich, the 2nd of June, 1553. A

letter to the Lord Russell, Lord Windesour, and the rest of the gentlemen within the Countie of Buckingham, in favour of Mr. Knockes, the preacher, according to the minutes."

Two leading members of the Council at this time, the Earl of Bedford and Sir Thomas Cheyne, were intimately associated with South Bucks. Cheyne belonged to the old Lollard stock already more than once referred to. It is noticeable that Knox seems to have begun his labours near Bedford's seat of Chenies. He may very likely have been entertained at the old manor-house, still standing, which was built a few years before his visit, and perhaps at Lord Windsor's seat at Bradenham. The Lord Russell to whom he was commended was probably Lord Francis, afterwards the second Earl, a man who not only staunchly supported the cause of Protestantism, but also cherished the traditions of the older reforming movement. At his death in 1585, when he left sums of money for "godly sermons" to be preached in Chenies Church and elsewhere he bequeathed his MSS. of Wycliffe's works, as a valued possession, to his friend Lord Burleigh; and in the Countess Cowper's library at Wrest Park is a vellum folio of Wycliffe's sermons, copied about 1400, bearing the autograph "Francis Russell" and the date 1556.

Knox left London with forebodings gloomy as Jonah's when he cried, "Yet forty days, and Nineveh shall be destroyed." He saw that the death of Edward meant the accession of Mary,

an alliance with her uncle Charles V. of Germany,
and a deadly blow to the Protestant cause throughout Europe. We have scarcely any definite
records of his work in Buckinghamshire. It commenced, as we have seen, early in June, and he
was back again in London on the 19th of July.
But he had visited the city during the interval,
for the earliest of his published letters is dated
from London on the 23rd of June. On
the 6th of July the young King died. The
unprincipled attempt of Northumberland to set
upon the throne Lady Jane Grey, whom he had
married to his son Lord Guildford Dudley during
Edward's illness, roused the spirit of the nation
on behalf of Mary. The county of Bucks, both
Catholic and Protestant, was enthusiastically in
her favour, and the boroughs of Wycombe, Aylesbury, and Buckingham, owed their charters of
incorporation to the loyalty they displayed in her
cause at this time. Sir Edward Hastings, of
Denham, had raised the musters of the county
in Mary's name, and had been joined by Sir
Thomas Wharton, of Upper Winchendon, and
by Sir Edmund Peckham, Cofferer of the Household, who had abandoned the court of the
" Twelfth Day Queen " with the treasure under
his charge. Knox knew that in opposing Mary's
succession he would speak at the peril of his life
from the troopers of Hastings; while even his
Protestant hearers would be offended at the interference of a foreigner with the claims of their
liege lady. But " he that never feared the face

of man," as the Regent Morton called him, was
not to be restrained by such considerations.
Wherever he went, he declared "that the last
trumpet was then in blowing within the realm
of England, and therefore ought every man to
prepare himself for battle. For if the trumpet
should altogether cease and be put to silence, it
should never blow again with the like force within the said realm, till the coming of the Lord
Jesus."

On Sunday, July 16th, just before his return
to London, Knox preached in Amersham Church.
Among his hearers there might be survivors of
the Lollards who had been branded on the cheek
and forced to do penance in the dark days of
persecution, which he now foresaw were about
to return, little as his hearers realised their danger. Writing at Dieppe, two years later, he calls
to mind the agitated scene ; and in his *Admonition
unto the Professors of God's Truth in England*,
he makes the following reference to it, with the
marginal heading, "What was sayd in Hammer-
shame, when uproure was for establyshing of
Marye in authority" :—

"In wrytinge herof it came to mind that after
the death of that innocent and moste godlye
kynge, Edwarde the Sixte, whyle that great
tumulte was in Englande for the establyshing of
that most unhappye and wycked womane's
authoritie (I mean of her that now raigneth in
Goddes wrath), entreatinge the same argument in
a towne in Buckinghamshyre, named Hammer-

shame, before a great congregation, with sorrowful herte and wepynge eyes, I fel into this exclamation :—

" ' O Englande! now is Goddes wrath kyndled againste thee. Nowe hath he begonne to punyshe, as he hath threatened a longe whyle, by his true prophetes and messengers. He hath taken from thee the crowne of thy glorie, and hath left thee without honour, as a bodye without a heade. And this appeareth to be onely the begynnynge of sorowes, which appeareth to encrease. For I perceave that the herte, the tounge, and the hande of one Englysh man is bente agaynst another, and devision to be in the whole realme, which is an assured signe of desolation to come.

" ' O Englande, Englande! doest thou not consider that thy common wealth is lyke a shippe sailyng on the sea; yf thy maryners and governours shall one consume another, shalte thou not suffer shipwracke in processe of tyme?

" ' O Englande, Englande! alasse! these plagues are powred upon thee, for that thou wouldest not knowe the moste happy tyme of thy gentle visitation. But wilt thou yet obey the voyce of thy God, and submitte thy selfe to his holy words? Truely, yf thou wilt, thou shalt fynde mercye in his syght, and the estate of thy common wealth shall be preserved.

" ' But, O Englande, Englande! yf thou obstinately wilt returne into Egypt, that is, yf thou contract mariage, confederacy, or league with

such princes as do mayntayne and advaunce
ydolatrie (such as the Emperoure, which is no
less enemie unto Christe than ever was Nero)
yf for the pleasure and friendshippe (I say) of
such princes, thou returne to thyne olde abhomi-
nations, before used under the Papistrie, then
assuredly, O Englande, thou shalt be plagued,
and brought to destruction, by the meanes of
those whose favoures thou sekest, and by whome
thou art procured to fall from Christ, and to serve
Anti-Christ.'

"This, and muche more, in the dolour of
myne herte, that day, in audience of such as yet
may beare recorde, God wolde that I should pro-
nounce. The thinge that I then most feared,
and which also my tounge spake—that is, the
subversion of the true religion, and bryngynge
in of straungers to raigne over that realme—this
day I see come to passe in men's counsels and
determinations." (Works, iii. 307-309).

It was in vain that the "Twelfth Day Queen"
ordered Sir John St. Lowe and Sir Anthony
Kingston to repair to Buckinghamshire and quell
the disturbances there. When Knox returned
to London, on July 19th, he found the city filled
with "fires of joy and riotous banquetings" at
the accession of Mary.

It would seem that his was not the only voice
uplifted at Amersham against the new order of
things. Foxe makes no mention of his sermon
(though it is alluded to by Strype); but in the
Acts and Monuments (vi. 392, 393) we read that

on August 16th, just a fortnight after Mary's entry into London, and upon the very day that Rogers and Bradford were imprisoned, " a letter was sent to the Sheriffs of Buckingham and Bedford, for the apprehending of one Fisher, parson of Amersham, a preacher " (John Fisher, S.T.B., who had held the living since 1544). On the 22nd, the day of Northumberland's execution on Tower Hill, " Fisher, parson of Amersham, made his appearance before the Council, and was appointed the next day to bring in a note of his sermon." Probably he submitted, but became once more a Protestant at Elizabeth's accession five years later, for he held the living till 1570. It seems strange that Knox should have escaped a similar reprimand, especially as, though in Kent at the time, he was in London again a month later. But his words were not forgotten ; and when later on, he had to leave the Imperial city of Frankfort, it was owing to his bold denunciation of the Emperor at Amersham.

The evil days which he had spoken of were not long in coming. The ecclesiastical laws of Edward VI. were repealed in December, but it was not till the close of the following year that the laws against Lollardy were re-enacted. It should never be forgotten that thirty-seven members, Catholics as well as Protestants, and numbering among them the great lawyer Plowden, withdrew from the House of Commons, to their eternal honour be it recorded, rather than sanction Mary's intolerant policy. Among the list of names given by Strype is that of " Thomas Moor, of Hambleton " (Hambleden), " Bucks," in the old Lollard district—a worthy precursor of John Hampden and other liberty-loving Buckingham-shire squires in the next century.

On the outbreak of Wyatt's rebellion in 1554, the Princess Elizabeth, who was at Ashridge, was brought up to London at the Queen's command by Lord William Howard, Sir Edward Hastings, and Sir Thomas Constable. Foxe's account of the harsh treatment she received is not borne out by the documentary evidence, from which it appears that she was brought up to London by easy stages on account of her illness, and treated with every consideration. She was committed to the Tower, but was soon sent to Woodstock, and then to Hampton Court. On her journey to and from Woodstock she passed through Buckinghamshire, and was greeted with respectful sympathy by the Protestant party. On each occasion she stayed one night at the ancient seat of the Dormers at Wing, and on the later journey slept at the George Inn at Colnbrook.

We may pass the more readily over the perse-cutions of the three following years, because their rage does not seem to have extended to Bucking-hamshire. John Taylor, who had become Bishop of Lincoln in 1552, on the death of Longland's successor Holbeach, had refused to attend mass at the Queen's coronation, and was deprived of his see. He would perhaps have shared the fate of Cranmer, Ridley, and Latimer, but for his

death soon after at his Buckinghamshire residence of Ankerwyke. His successors, John
White (translated to Winchester in 1556) and
Thomas Watson, seem to have been merciful
men ; for only two appear to have suffered in all
their vast diocese, and it is said that one of these
was burned at the instigation of Cardinal Pole.
It is significant that the greater number of the
Marian martyrs, among the laity at any rate,
came from Lollard counties. This is well shown
in the maps of Rev. W. H. Beckett's *English
Reformation* (R.T.S., 1890).

Three victims suffered as near the Bucks border as the Lynch Green at Uxbridge—John
Denley and Robert Smith, on the 8th of August,
1555, and Patrick Packingham on the 28th of
the same month.

On a brass of Elizabeth's time, preserved in
Beaconsfield Church, are the following lines,
which Foxe (vii. 369) says were written by Robert
Smith in Newgate :—

Content thyself with patience
    With Christ to bear the cross of pain,
Which can and will thee recompense
    A thousandfold with lyke again.
Let nothing cause thy heart to quail ;
    Launch out thy boote, haule up thy sail,
      Put from the shore ;
And at the length thou shalt attain
    Unto the port that shall remain
      For evermore.

At last, in November, 1558, the Fiery Terror of the Marian persecution was brought to a close by the death of Mary on one day and of Pole on the next. Immediately on the accession of Elizabeth, a " Commission of Lollardy," which had been issued by Philip and Mary in 1556, was called on to give in its report, but it was only in order to stay further proceedings. Early in 1559 the acts against Lollardy were finally repealed ; although, as we have seen, an oath against it continued to be taken by magistrates till 1625.

Our narrative has now reached the close of the Lollard period, and we have only to refer to the way in which Lollardy has influenced the subsequent religious history of the district we have had in mind. This has been singularly marked. The Lollard spirit, like the Lollard traditions, has never entirely died out of its old haunts among the Chilterns. It showed itself in the yeomen who marched to London to protect John Hampden on the threatened arrest of the Five Members, and in the Greencoats who marched under the same patriot's banner, with its haughty motto, *Vestigia nulla retrorsum*. It showed itself not less clearly in the patient endurance of persecution by the early Baptists, and by the peaceful Quakers whose remains lie beneath the linden-trees of Jordans, and many of the peculiarities of both these sects may be traced back to the Lollards. It shows itself to this day in the deep-rooted love of religious freedom which marks the inhabitants of some of the upland villages, a love ingrained in their very nature by the habits and traditions of half-a-thousand years.

A very surprising statement appeared in a letter to the *Academy* of April, 15th, 1893, by Mr. Wentworth Webster. He says :—

"In the year 1849 or 1850 I was laid up for a week from an accident in riding at a lonely farm-house, Row Wood, between Chalfont St. Giles and Chenies. The old woman who waited on me, the only inmate of the house except a friend of the same age as myself, called herself an Old Methodist. I soon discovered that she looked upon the reformed Church of England as a comparatively modern sect, and asserted that the body to which she belonged had received the Gospel long before, and that they were descendants of the old Lollards. She indignantly repudiated any connection with Wesley's Methodism. The only books in the house were two or three tracts belonging to the old woman. These I read. The oldest of them dated from the last century, and referred to an attempt of Lady Huntingdon to include these Old or Primitive Methodists in her Connexion. Her advances had been repelled, and the same statement made which the old woman repeated to me. This small sect had then some kind of chapel or meeting-room in Chalfont and in Amersham, and was said to be more numerous in the counties bordering on Wales. How far this is historically true, or whether the little body, with its traditions of descent from the Lollards still exists, I cannot say. Only I distinctly assert that such a body making such claims did exist, both in the last century and about 1850.''

There are several points in Mr. Webster's account, and especially his use of the term '' Primitive Methodists,'' which would suggest to those most familiar with Nonconformist history that he must have misunderstood the old lady and her tracts. Nor have I been able to discover any trace or memory of the sect he describes ; while the old lady herself appears to have been a respected member of the Congregational church at Chalfont St. Giles ! Still I am far from asserting that all his statements are erroneous ; and it is a curious fact that both in the Tenison MSS. in the Lambeth Library, and in the Browne Willis MSS. in the Bodleian, there are vague indications of the existence of some peculiar sect at Chalfont St. Giles in the seventeenth and eighteenth centuries.

But the most lasting heritage bequeathed by the Lollards is not to be found in sects and denominations, or even in doctrinal protests against Romish error, but in the yet unspent moral force which resulted from their life and work. For after all, their protest was quite as much ethical as doctrinal. The striking words of Archbishop Trench in his *Lectures on Mediæval Church History* (p. 259) are almost as applicable to the English Lollards as to the Waldenses :—

" If any one turns to these authoritative writings of the Waldenses, expecting to find in them
the fulness and freeness of the Pauline teaching
on the propitiatory work of Christ, or the forgive-
ness of sin on our justification by faith in Him,
he will be disappointed. He will find the supremacy of Holy Scripture asserted as against every
teaching and tradition of men ; but the prevailing
type of doctrine is more that of St. James than
that of St. Paul. Nor is this very strange. That,
as we have seen, which constituted the very heart
and kernel of the Waldensian movement was not
opposition to any doctrine taught in the Church
of Rome, but a desire, first stirred up through
the reading of the Holy Scriptures, after the
highest form of Christian life, and that nearest
to the apostolic ideal. Only by degrees, and not
until they had been cast out, did the Waldenses
discover that doctrinally also much was amiss in
that body which had so violently separated them
from itself. And even then it was the corruptions
standing in the way of a high and holy living
which called forth their strongest protests—indulgences, Purgatory . . . . . it was these and
similar abuses, abating as they did the moral
earnestness with which men should work out
their salvation, which aroused their most indig-
nant remonstrances.''

The Lollards were pioneers in the path of
religious, social, and political reform. All England owes them a debt of gratitude for the liberties
which they purchased with their blood and tears,

and not the least should the county of Buckingham honour their memory along with those of
the worthies associated with her story at a
later day—Hampden and Sydney, Milton and
Penn.